AMC GUIDE TO
Winter Hiking & Camping

AMC GUIDE TO
Winter Hiking & Camping

Everything You Need to Plan Your
Next Cold-Weather Adventure

Yemaya Maurer & Lucas St. Clair

Appalachian Mountain Club Books
Boston, Massachusetts

The AMC is a nonprofit organization and sales of AMC books fund our mission of protecting the Northeast outdoors. If you appreciate our efforts and would like to make a donation, contact us at Appalachian Mountain Club Books, 5 Joy Street, Boston, MA 02108.

http://www.outdoors.org/publications/books/

Book design by Eric Edstam

Illustrations © Tenaya Gordon

Library of Congress Cataloging-in-Publication Data
Maurer, Yemaya.
   AMC guide to winter hiking and camping : everything you need to plan your next cold-weather adventure / Yemaya Maurer and Lucas St. Clair.
     p. cm.
   Includes bibliographical references and index.
   ISBN 978-1-934028-12-4 (alk. paper)
   1. Snow camping. 2. Snow camping—Equipment and supplies. 3. Hiking. I. St. Clair, Lucas. II. Title.

   GV198.9.M314 2008
   796.54—dc22

                              2008021164

 Printed on 100% recycled post-consumer fiber.
Printed in Canada

10 9 8 7 6 5 4 3 2 1   09 10 11 12 13 14 15 16

Contents

Introduction

I confess: I used to think sleeping outside in the deep cold of winter was just about as miserable as life gets. Sure, I loved long day hikes through snowy landscapes, but much of the fun came from the knowledge that my efforts would be rewarded once I reached home—land of heat, hot water, and puffy down comforters. Then a nature-loving boyfriend convinced me to give winter camping a try.

Although I made a few rookie mistakes that first night—it hadn't occurred to me that boots, left outside overnight, could freeze—I was floored by how much I enjoyed the experience. The heavy snowpack offered endless opportunities for creating a plush campsite, complete with wind-blocking walls, tent platforms, benches, kitchen counters, and cabinets. And there were no bugs! By the time the purple alpenglow settled into darkness that night and the moon rose, casting long shadows, I knew I had found my new favorite season—winter.

I met my future husband and co-author, Lucas, on a semester-long mountaineering course in Patagonia, Chile, in 1998. Our friendship blossomed over long hikes across snowfields and glaciers. As we continued traveling through Chile, both our winter hiking skills and relationship developed. Since then, our love for winter camping has taken us everywhere from the wet Northern Cascades to the dry Colorado Rockies and from the majestic peaks of Alaska to the rolling mountains of New Hampshire.

Over the years, I have come to realize that my winter hiking and camping skills are applicable to outdoor adventures during the other three seasons. On more than one high country journey, early or late summer snowstorms have caught me by surprise. My winter camping experiences have taught me to be fully prepared, efficient, resourceful, and mindful of myself and my gear during these unexpected situations.

I started teaching winter hiking and camping skills to children and teenagers in 2002. Until then, I often mourned the missed winter adventures of my youth—if only I had known what is was like to sit on snow-carved benches around a crackling fire or wake to fresh powder! Now, every time I dig a snow cave or slide down steep slopes on the tails of my snowshoes, I feel I'm reclaiming a slice of the childhood experiences I never had. And when I help self-conscious 15-year-olds successfully start a fire after many failed attempts, cook a delicious outdoor meal for the first time in their lives, or set up a taught tarp for shelter, I feel a surge of satisfaction that is difficult to find in other environments. I hope this book helps you enjoy some of the same delights.

—*Yemaya Maurer*

For me, winter camping has always been a way of life. I grew up in the North Woods of Maine in a log cabin my parents built that lacked electricity, running water, and other modern conveniences. Before many kids have even built a snowman, my twin sister and I were camping out in the backyard snow fort, which was often warmer than our drafty cabin.

My most cherished moments have been crawling into a sleeping bag, cinching it down over my face, and falling asleep warm and happy. I've always been a cold-weather person, and I feel that anyone can enjoy winter outings as much as I do. All it takes is a bit of knowledge, the right gear, and an open mind.

I gained a lot of outdoor experience while hiking the Appalachian Trail and paddling the Northern Forest Canoe Trail—a 900-mile scenic waterway stretching from New York to Maine. I honed my skills during a challenging National Outdoor Leadership School semester in Patagonia, Chile, during which I met Yemaya. I also learned a lot during day hikes and overnight trips close to home in Maine. Whether camping out in the backyard or trekking across foreign lands, the best time to be outdoors is often in the winter—the landscape is quiet, the frozen waterways offer a surface to travel on, and you can reach areas that are entirely inaccessible in warmer months.

This book is dedicated to helping you discover the joys of winter hiking and camping. It thoroughly covers the basics, taking you through the steps of planning, organizing, and conducting a fun, successful trip. So, go ahead, ditch your old hibernation habits, and embrace the wintry world. You'll be surprised by how warm, comfortable, and spectacular it can be.

—*Lucas St. Clair*

Acknowledgments

We thank the many wonderful teachers we've had on the winter trails, including the students of Gould Academy and the Student Conservation Association. For introducing us to technical winter camping skills—and to each other—we are deeply indebted to the National Outdoor Leadership School. Lorenzo Baker, our friend and mentor, showed us how to travel and live well among organized chaos, and we are particularly grateful for his patience, generosity, and good humor. Were it not for The Quimby Family Foundation and Great Aunt Lily, we would never have secured this book deal. This book would not have the beautiful illustrations it has were it not for the dedication and commitment of the talented Tenaya Gordon. Tenaya stepped into this project at a crucial moment and we are forever grateful for all she contributed. Some of the photos in this book were captured by friends, who also happen to be great photographers. In particular, we would like to thank Sarah and Ethan Hipple and Halsey Bell. Thanks are also due to our editor, Dan Eisner, who helped transform a raw manuscript into the book you hold in your hands. More than anything, we are thankful to our wonderful families who continue encouraging and inspiring us to journey forth.

CHAPTER ONE
Winter Hiking and Camping Basics

Cold does not penetrate, though that figure of speech is appealing. It is heat, the positive, which flows outward, and cold is its negative condition.
—Excerpted from *Winter Camping* (1913), the first book
published on "The New Sport" of winter camping

It's cold out there. It might even be freezing, or below freezing. You might be tempted to hole up indoors, counting down the months until the snow will melt, the temperature will rise, and you will be able to return to your favorite trails. But if you have ever spent a winter afternoon building snowmen or lobbing snowballs at your friends, you know how invigorating the cold, fresh air feels in your lungs. You've heard the satisfying squeak of fresh snow beneath your boots, and you've seen sunlight dance across fallen snow and frozen ponds. Haven't you wondered what your favorite trails look like blanketed in white? Haven't you wanted to go outside and explore?

All you really need to get started is a spirit of adventure. You don't need to attempt to climb Mount Everest on your first outing; just get comfortable playing in the snow in your backyard. Soon you'll be hitting your favorite local trails and experiencing them in a whole new way. You may even develop a desire to camp overnight in the snow. Go ahead—give it a try! As long as you know how to keep yourself warm and dry, you'll discover that winter camping is easier and more enjoyable than you would ever imagine. Winter hiking and camping has its challenges, of course, but you can meet them head on if you simply plan ahead and prepare. If you're ready to pull hiking boots back out of the closet, bundle up, and head out the door, keep reading. You'll thank yourself later.

Staying Warm and Dry

In order to survive and thrive in the wintry outdoors, staying warm and dry is essential. Let this be your mantra. Avid outdoor enthusiasts tend to love top-of-the-line equipment—they may even tell you that it's the key to successful winter camping—but gear alone won't assure dry warmth. You have to know how to maintain and utilize it to reap its benefits. Good equipment, while useful, is not as crucial as proper attire, good health, and eating and drinking plenty. And gear won't help when it comes to basic backcountry skills, such as navigation and outdoor cooking. A Global Positioning System (GPS) and an ultra-light cook stove do you no good (and may weigh you down) if they fail to work properly or you don't know how to use them. New technology, gear, and materials have their place, but other things are far more critical to ensuring warmth and dryness.

As you read this book, you'll learn everything you should know about staying warm and dry, from the clothes to wear to the food to eat to how to build snow shelters without getting wet. Many techniques are for particular situations that you may never face, so here are our favorite general tips for staying warm and dry on every outing:

Winter hiking allows you to explore remote areas such as the Cascade Mountains, pictured here.

- *Cut the cotton.* Cotton quickly absorbs moisture (just think about your plush bathroom towels). You don't want anything close to your body that retains moisture, so leave your blue jeans, T-shirts, and jersey socks at home.
- *Sweat stinks.* It actually does more than stink—it makes you wet. If you sweat and get soaked, you will lose heat. When moving, it's better to be cool and dry than hot and sweaty, so layer up or down depending on the conditions and your activity level, which leads us to the next point.
- *Love your layers.* Multiple layers of thin clothing are much better than one super thick Michelin Man suit. If you get hot, simply take off a layer or two. If you get cold, put them back on. With the Michelin Man suit, you won't be able to take anything off if you get too hot.

This cross-country skier wears non-cotton clothing, including a synthetic long underwear shirt, a fleece pull-over, and waterproof/breathable shell pants.

- *If your feet are cold, put on a hat.* Your body loses a lot of heat through your head and neck if they aren't covered. When your body starts to get cold, it draws blood away from the extremities (such as the feet and hands) in order to keep its vital organs warm. Putting on a hat will help you retain the heat.
- *Brush off the snow.* Brush off any clothing or part of your body that gets covered with snow if you accidentally fall down. The warmth from your body will quickly melt the snow and make you wet if you fail to get it off as soon as possible.
- *Eat!* Eat at least twice as much as you would normally eat at home. Snack at every break. Embrace high-calorie, high-fat foods.
- *Drink!* Hydration is the key to maintaining warmth, so drink water at a disciplined rate throughout the day. Don't eat snow to get hydrated; turning water from a solid to a liquid state requires a significant amount of energy and you won't have that much energy to spare. Check your urine to see if you're hydrated—if your urine is clear and copious, you're in good shape. If not, drink up!
- *Pack a little more.* Whether on a quick day hike or a multiday camping trip, you'll need to carry more food, water, and clothing than you would at any other time of year. Winter is not the season to try your hand at ultra-light hiking!

Leave No Trace

If you've ever ventured into the backcountry and seen it littered with candy wrappers or scarred with fire rings, you know that humans can have a negative impact on the pristine places we visit. Although our wild lands have been treated poorly, we're also making great strides to conserve them for future generations. People are becoming familiar with the slogan "Take only pictures, leave only footprints," thanks to the combined efforts of the Leave No Trace Center for Outdoor Ethics, the National Outdoor Leadership School, and multiple land management agencies. The Leave No Trace (LNT) educational programs and guidelines, based on seven principles (detailed below), are helping hikers and campers contribute to responsible stewardship of the land.

Some winter enthusiasts incorrectly assume that the LNT principles don't apply in the winter, arguing that snow will eventually melt away any sign of human impact. It's true that you can travel on snow without leaving a trace, but remember that any solid waste you leave behind—from apple cores to feces—won't begin to decompose until the snow melts. It's good practice in the winter to follow the LNT principles the same way you would during the other three seasons, keeping in mind that the principles are guidelines—not rules—to help you enjoy the wilderness and protect it.

Familiarize yourself and your group members with the LNT principles before you head into the backcountry. If working with youth, present the principles in a structured but fun format that promotes enthusiasm for minimizing human impact on the land. We often have young people teach each other the principles, then perform skits or act out scenarios to demonstrate correct LNT practices.

1. *Plan Ahead and Prepare.* Planning ahead and preparing entail learning about the area you intend to visit and packing to minimize the amount of waste you bring into the backcountry. Research the local regulations: If fires are prohibited in the area you plan to visit, you better know that in advance; if the land management agency expects you to carry out your own excrement, you better have the proper bags and materials to do so.

When packing your food, repackage it from its original cardboard or cellophane packaging, and put it in plastic bags. After consuming the food, you can use the bags to store your garbage. This will reduce the amount of trash you have to carry.

2. *Travel and Camp on Durable Surfaces.* Because land does not get damaged when people hike on snow, the snow is considered a durable surface. Travel

By following the Leave No Trace principles and camping on snow and rock, you will minimize impact on the land.

on snow as much as possible and if you can, camp on snow that is at least 2 feet deep. When setting up camp, try to avoid digging all the way down to the ground. During the winter, many small mammals live in narrow tunnels they dig along the ground under the snow. If for some reason you remove that layer of snow, be sure to replace it before leaving camp.

If an area lacks adequate snow, look for other durable surfaces, such as rock, gravel, sand, and grass. If designated campsites are in the area, use those. If not, camp in a well-established site where people have obviously camped before. If you see no evidence of past campers, such as flattened vegetation or a fire ring, choose a durable surface, such as rock, sand, gravel or dried grasses, and do your best to minimize your impact there. Never build "furniture" with logs and rocks or rearrange the landscape to suit your fancy. And always camp away from the trail and at least 200 feet from water sources.

3. Dispose of Waste Properly. We're all familiar with the phrase "Pack it in, pack it out," a phrase that holds merit in every season and wilderness area. To ensure you pack it all out, have garbage bags on hand and always do a sweep of the area where you camped or stopped to rest. Pick up everything from candy wrappers to apple cores and orange peels. Some people incorrectly think discarded organic materials do no harm to the environment. In fact, food waste attracts scavengers, which often drive away native animals.

When it comes to human waste (urine and feces) you usually don't have to pack it out, but you do have to be mindful of where you do your business, particularly when it comes to poop. Nobody will want to stumble upon a pile of human feces when they go on their first spring hike. When possible, use trailhead and backcountry toilets. If that's not an option, dig a hole through the snow and 6 inches into the ground at the base of a tree, defecate there, and cover it up. Be careful when approaching the bases of trees, as some have depressed snow, called tree wells, that you could sink into if you aren't careful (see Chapter 10 for a discussion on tree wells). In a treeless land, try to find a large boulder and dig a hole next to it. If the area is completely barren, just dig in an area away from camp, water, and other people. Defecate at least 200 feet from any water source. On the other hand, feel free to urinate on the snow wherever you'd like. But consider designating a pee tree at camp so that you don't have unsightly yellow patches everywhere you look.

One of the most important things to remember is to pack out your non-organic waste, such as used feminine hygiene products and toilet paper (if you use it—many prefer snow). We always carry a few small, empty Ziploc bags in our pockets for this purpose. When we fill a bag, we double bag it inside another plastic bag, tuck it deep into a corner of our pack, and dispose of it as soon as we return home. When we lead teenagers, we give each young woman her own duct tape-covered Ziploc bag so that she can add items to it without feeling self-conscious about another group member seeing its contents.

4. *Leave What You Find.* In the backcountry, people often are tempted to either leave their mark or take a souvenir. The goal of Leave No Trace is for people to leave the backcountry as they found it. Do not carve your initials into a tree or scratch them on rocks; nor should you take fossils, bones, or artifacts home to add to your collection. If you do find an artifact, such as an arrowhead, pottery, or a tool, mark on your map where you found it, and leave it there. Notify the agency in charge of managing that land about your discovery when you've returned to the front country.

5. *Minimize Campfire Impacts.* Many places do not permit campfires because the area has been damaged by heavy use or the environment is particularly sensitive. In places where they are allowed, it may not be easy to find enough suitable, dry wood to maintain a fire. Where fires are allowed and wood is plentiful, build a small, minimum-impact fire using only dead and downed wood no thicker than your wrist. Avoid building fires next to rock outcrops, as black scars on rocks remain for many years. Burn the fire completely down to put it out and then, before leaving camp, widely disperse the cool ash. By keeping a fire small and dispersing its remains, you will ensure that the area remains pristine for future hikers and campers.

These teens enjoy the small campfire they built at their campsite near the White Mountains, Maine.

6. *Respect Wildlife.* You should take special care during the winter, when animals are weaker than in summer months, to minimize your contact with wildlife. Observe animals from a distance, keep still and quiet, and stay away from dens and nesting sites. Never feed wildlife directly or indirectly by leaving behind food scraps. Unlike during the warmer months, when you may store your food at night in many places, you do not need to be so cautious during winter. However, it's always a good idea to check with the land use agency in the region where you are traveling, as some require you to put your food in protective bear bags throughout the year—bears do occasionally become active in the winter.

Bring pets only if the recreational area allows them. Keep your dog nearby and under control, and use a leash if your dog does not immediately respond to voice commands. Even where dogs are allowed, consider leaving them at home when you venture into the backcountry. Some other winter travelers (including wildlife) may not appreciate your dog's company. You might also find that traveling without your pet allows you to focus better on your surroundings and yourself.

7. *Be Considerate of Other Visitors.* Because fewer people hike and camp in the winter, you will be sharing the wilderness with few other people. However, you will occasionally encounter other people. Practice trail etiquette: let faster skiers and snowshoers pass; resist the urge to mess up a well-established ski track; and take rest breaks at least 10 feet from the trail. When setting up camp, do your best to stay away from the trail and other campers, and keep your noise to a minimum.

Winter Ecology

The winter heightens sensory awareness and rewards an appreciation for contrast and subtle sounds. As a result, naturalists find the ecosystem just as spectacular and diverse during the winter as it is at other times of the year. The winter sky provides a canvas for excellent stargazing, as nights are often clear and fewer dust particles pollute the air than during warmer seasons. The constellation Orion (the mighty hunter) stands prominently, taking up the southern region of the winter sky in the Northern Hemisphere. Around sunset, it's often possible to see Venus or Mercury low in the western sky. Animal tracks are more visible in the snow, though wildlife sightings are less frequent. The shorter days offer less light for animals to forage, and finding food is more challenging because of the snow cover and the cold. This sends many animals into hibernation and many plants into dormancy, lowering the food supply. Different species have adapted in various ways: some hibernate or migrate south; others change their diet and grow thicker hair or a more dense covering of feathers; still others modify their behavior, employing such tactics as huddling for warmth or shivering to stave off the cold.

The secret to viewing wildlife in the winter is to understand what the non-migrating and non-hibernating animals eat when the temperature drops. Pay close attention to cedar trees, as their berries provide nourishment for as many as 63 bird species, along with deer and mice. In forests where pines are plentiful, look for chickadees, blue jays, juncos, grosbeaks, sparrows, and cardinals. One of the more delightful treats for the winter hiker is the glimpse of a red cardinal against the pale winter sky. Mammals, such as raccoons and red and gray squirrels, also frequent coniferous woods. In oak and beech tree forests, keep your eye out for dry, hollow, or abandoned trees, which are often the winter homes of eastern gray squirrels and other small mammals. Red foxes prefer bedding down in open fields or on south-facing slopes while eastern cottontail, which feed on sumac, maple, oak, and blackberry, make their homes in pastures and dense thickets.

Bring a good field guide into the backcountry if you have the room and are willing to carry the extra weight. We always find our experience enhanced when we take the time to look carefully at our environment and appreciate how other living entities are coping with the cold. Sometimes we leave our field guides at home, but carry a small waterproof notebook and a pencil so that we can take notes and draw pictures of our observations. To help with plant identification, we look at branch patterns, bark, twigs, seed containers, and stalks, and we draw pictures of each of those characteristics. Then, once home, we scour through resources to figure out what we saw in the backcountry. It's one of many ways we continue the adventure long after we've left the field.

CHAPTER TWO

Trip Planning

If you live in a cold climate, you're familiar with how to brace yourself against the chill with a hat, gloves, warm clothes, and a belly full of hearty food. Dressing well and eating plenty are at the core of every successful cold-weather adventure, and the ability to cope with winter's harshness is testament to a person's skills. Even if you possess those skills, don't rush out to the woods just yet. Travel on the snowy trail is different from the jaunt between your car and office.

Where to Go

One of the best ways to build skills and confidence is to start close to home. If you've never built a snow fort or pitched a tent in your snowy backyard, give it a try. Children, in particular, are much more comfortable in the snowy woods if they have already enjoyed building snowmen and snow shelters. Some of our friends take backyard snow play to the extreme and build a huge snow luge in the hilly pasture behind their house every winter. Their small children rode the luge on inner tubes (sitting in their parents' laps, of course) before they could walk; once they'd grown a bit, they were begging their parents to take them out on winter hikes.

Local Destinations

Venture outside your neighborhood in winter by visiting local parks and nature centers, some of which offer guided winter hikes and provide you the gear and instruction you need, regardless of your experience. At the Boston Nature Center and Wildlife Sanctuary, for example, naturalists offer guided snowshoe walks along the center's two miles of trails. Hikers borrow snowshoes and pay a nominal fee to support the center and learn about the migratory birds and

Enjoying the ride down a homemade luge in New Hampshire, these winter enthusiasts prove that winter fun can often be found right outside the front door.

coyotes that visit the sanctuary. Hikes such as these are great introductions into the snowy world outside your back door.

When you're ready to go guideless, consider revisiting the trails close to home that you frequent in the warmer months. Most people who take up winter hiking and camping are experienced three-season outdoor enthusiasts who are tired of storing away their boots and sleeping bags when the weather turns cold. If you fall into this category, you're probably already familiar with the trails in your area and have favorite destinations you return to repeatedly in the fall, spring, and summer. Why not see what they're like in winter? Practicing in familiar areas close to home offers the freedom to experiment with food and

This day-hiker warms up her winter legs on a short hike close to her home.

gear in a familiar environment where you will have the comfort of knowing you can easily go home. Not only will you save time, money, and gas by not traveling long distances, you may also find local wilderness adventures very rewarding.

When we help beginners plan their first winter hiking trip, we always have to pull in the reins on their ambitious mileage goals. People often think that if they were easily doing 8-mile day hikes before snow blanketed the ground, they should be able to do the same in winter. We explain that snow going is slow going, especially for beginners who are learning about new gear and how to stay warm without overheating. And then there's the fact that the days are much shorter during the winter than the summer, so you will not be able to hike as many hours. We recommend 3-mile day hikes for beginning winter travelers, regardless of the amount of hiking they have done in warm weather.

As you venture into the woods, you'll want to see what's around the bend. You'll be tempted to go farther and higher, as we were on this trail in Washington's Cascade Range.

Venturing Out Overnight

After a few day hikes, you'll probably want to travel farther and stay out longer. Overnight winter camping trips give hikers the opportunity to travel greater distances and intimately experience the wintry woods. Great winter camping may be right outside your doorstep, so consider starting close to home.

For those wanting to transition into winter camping with ease, we suggest starting with a hut trip. Huts provide the opportunity to take an overnight hiking trip without having to carry your own shelter. Examples of great transitional overnight trips include snowshoe and cross-country ski journeys to the AMC's popular White Mountain destinations of Lonesome Lake Hut and Zealand Falls Hut. The round-trip distance to and from Lonesome Lake Hut is 3.2 miles,

The backcountry offers a big, pristine world that's all yours to explore.

offering the most accessible and family friendly hut in the Northeast. Zealand Falls Hut (9.3 miles round-trip) is a more ambitious destination, but skiers are rewarded for their effort with spectacular views. Both huts operate on a self-service basis during winter, meaning guests bring food and sleeping bags but may use the huts' stoves, ovens, cookware, and bunk beds.

Once you become comfortable hiking near your home or spending an evening in the comfortable confines of a hut, you'll be ready to venture into the backcountry. Generally, the term "backcountry" refers to a region that is remote, undeveloped, and difficult to access, but backcountry enthusiasts would add that the backcountry has a pristine, magical quality unparalleled in developed lands. Others fear the backcountry—especially in the winter—as its remoteness does mean greater risk: trailheads are few and far between, roads are poorly maintained, and the comforts of civilization (including timely emergency medical care) lie far from the woods. It's healthy to fear the backcountry; a little fear keeps you aware of your surroundings and alert to its dangers. But if you explore the backcountry slowly—starting with day hikes—you can incrementally build upon your skills and experience until you're comfortable enjoying extended backcountry camping trips.

When to Go

After you decide to take an excursion into the backcountry, you'll need to choose a time. Any of the winter months will offer a satisfying experience, but late winter is an especially prime time—snow is piled high, the days are longer, and the temperatures have usually moderated by late February or early March. By this time, the likelihood of glimpsing wildlife is greater, as animals—like humans—respond to the increased light and warmth by venturing out.

A great benefit of winter hiking and camping is that the backcountry expands in the winter. Lakes, frozen solid, become choice terrain for quick traverses between points on opposite shores. Roads open in warmer months to motor traffic often go unplowed in the winter, offering prime highways for snowshoe hikes and ski tours. However, this can make reaching some backcountry destinations a challenge. Even with a high-clearance vehicle and snow tires or chains, it may be impossible to reach a trailhead without walking the last few miles. More than once, we've chosen a trail to hike and drove toward it, only to find several feet of uncleared snow miles before the parking lot, making it impossible to drive further. We've learned not to make assumptions. Instead, we seek out the best local source of information and start asking questions.

Gathering Information

Our research often begins on the Internet, where we browse backpackers' blogs, hiking club trail descriptions, and official management agency websites. Next, we scour the bookstore for guidebooks and maps of the area, keeping in mind that although books contain a huge amount of valuable information, they don't usually provide up-to-date information. Once we've narrowed our choices down to a few areas, we start making phone calls. Here is the arsenal of questions we pose to the land agency or organization most familiar with each area we are considering visiting:

- Is the road well maintained all the way to the trailhead?
- If not, how far from the trailhead is the road plowed?
- Is a four-wheel-drive vehicle recommended?
- Is there a close place to park so we can walk the remaining distance?
- Are tire chains recommended?

Answers to the above questions will help you determine whether you feel the destination you're considering is accessible. If you've concluded that the trailhead seems accessible, it's time to launch into the next round of questions:

Is the trailhead marked and easily visible? If not, find out what road or landscape features indicate where you will find the trailhead. If it seems that the trailhead will be too difficult to locate, choose a different one.

How much use does the trail get this time of year? Trails that are significantly traveled are generally easier to travel, as the trail is packed down and defined. However, popular trails mean more people, so don't expect solitude if you chose a well-traveled trail. If the trail doesn't get a lot of use during winter, you're more likely to find solitude, but less likely to find a packed trail; expect travel time to be slower.

Is it likely that we will be breaking trail or that the trail is already broken? Breaking trail takes more time than traveling on a packed one, and with fresh snow becomes even more difficult. If an area has received significant snowfall in the last few days and you expect to be breaking trail, prepare to travel at half the speed you normally would on a packed trail.

Does the route stay within a protected and forested area or is it exposed? Exposed routes may offer gorgeous views, but they do so at a cost—wind. If the forecast calls for high winds, avoid exposed routes. If you choose to travel exposed routes, be aware of protected areas near your route so that you can retreat to them in the event of a major storm (see Chapter 10).

Are there any unmarked hazards we should be aware of? Potential hazards include dead trees at risk of falling and snow-covered lakes and rivers that aren't frozen solid (see Chapter 10).

What is the weather forecast? Because winter weather can change quickly, you should always be prepared for poor weather by carrying the correct clothing and gear, eating ample food, and drinking plenty of water. However, you should still pay attention to the forecast. If a big storm is expected, postpone your trip. If the forecast calls for mild temperatures and calm weather, go out and enjoy—and leave the balaclava and puffy parka at home.

What is the depth and quality of the snow? Dry, fluffy powder can be difficult to plow through when it's deep, but it makes for fantastic descents when you're heading downhill. If a huge snowfall has recently occurred and the powder is deep, head to a trail that is well traveled so you won't have to break trail. If the snow is especially icy, avoid exposed ridges where the risk of slipping and falling is greater.

What are the avalanche conditions? If the avalanche risk is high, stay home. If risk is moderate, you should venture out only if you know how to assess the possibility that a slope will avalanche and know how to use the correct avalanche gear (a shovel, beacon, and probe; see Chapter 10 for more information about avalanches).

Have maps of the area on hand during these conversations. While U.S. Geological Survey topographical (topo) maps are standard for the backcountry, they are not always up-to-date and should be cross-referenced with multiple sources. Other maps—road maps, tourist maps, and maps published by local outfitters—can help provide a complete picture of the area you intend to visit. Use your topo map as your primary map, and pencil in any noteworthy additions you find from cross-referencing the other maps, reading guidebooks, and talking with local rangers. If you learn about hazards, lookout points, or archeological sites along your intended route, mark them directly on your primary map. For the tech-savvy, computer software allows for the creation of custom maps.

As you consider all the information, keep in mind the experience and fitness level of every person in your group, and involve them in trip planning. Less-experienced people often leave big decisions up to the seasoned party members. They fail to ask questions or voice their concerns and are then surprised when the backcountry experience is completely different from what they expected. Encourage everyone to contribute their thoughts, and ask them to speak up if they're uncomfortable with any proposed decision.

While planning your intended route, make sure everyone notes the mileage and elevation changes. Keep in mind that everything—from traveling and setting up camp to cooking and getting water—takes nearly twice as long in winter as it does in summer. You should have multiple destinations in mind and carefully weigh the pros and cons of each before settling on one. But no matter what, newcomers to winter hiking and camping should keep it simple during their first few trips:

- Limit yourself to familiar areas.
- Set realistic mileage goals (see Chapter 6).
- Choose a trail with short escape routes, in case the terrain or conditions don't meet your expectations and you need to retreat.
- Pick a straightforward route that doesn't require advanced map and compass skills, even if you are strong at navigation during the warmer months.
- Postpone the trip if the forecast calls for extreme weather conditions.

Even a thoroughly well-researched journey can present unforeseen challenges, so plan for contingencies. On your base map, note all the sheltered areas where you can find protection in case of a storm, and mark all the "bail out" points along your route. Knowing your alternatives in advance will allow you to change your plan or retreat before you get into trouble.

Permits and Regulations

After months of planning and growing excitement, you finally reach your backcountry destination, only to come face to face with a ranger who sends you home because you don't have the necessary permits to travel and camp there. Bummer. Sure, it may seem that all the permits and regulations are meant just to keep you from having a good time, but that's not the case; they exist to manage a fragile natural resource. By acquiring the necessary permits prior to venturing out, and by respecting the regulations once you're there, you'll minimize your impact and help ensure that these special places remain intact for the enjoyment of future generations.

Public lands that require a permit for daytime or overnight use during the summer usually enforce that requirement during the winter, too. Unlike during the summer, though, you probably won't need to reserve a permit months in advance, because you'll be one of a small number of people requesting the right to set up camp in the backcountry. However, it would be wise to contact the appropriate land management organization about permit requirements as soon as you've settled on your route.

Regulations often relax slightly in the winter because the ground, covered in snow, isn't as fragile as it is in warmer months. When the snow is deep enough to minimize any traveler's impact, you can often camp anywhere you like. On the flip side, you may not be able to camp—or travel—at all where you expected you could: some parks (especially state parks) lack the funding to stay open and maintained during the winter months. Take home point? Do your research.

Last-Minute Details

With so much planning to do, you may overlook those important last-minute details—such as winterizing your vehicle and checking your equipment—that can make or break a trip. If you haven't done extensive car travel in the winter, read the section about winter driving in your owner's manual. Then review the following list to ensure successful transportation to and from the trailhead:

- Treat your car to a basic tune-up before setting out.
- Check that the following are in good condition and (where applicable) at sufficient levels:
  1. Spark plugs
  2. Battery
  3. Antifreeze
  4. Belts

5. Oil

6. Gasoline

7. Washer fluid

- Decide whether to use chains, snow tires, and/or four-wheel drive. If you're using chains, make sure they're in good condition and that you've practiced putting them on and taking them off. If you've decided to use snow tires, put them on all four wheels to ensure that you get the best control.

- Properly inflate your tires.

- Pack the following accessories in your car—they'll definitely come in handy if your vehicle gets stuck in the snow or breaks down:

1. Shovel

2. Scrapers

3. Sack of sand and gravel

4. Flares

Later in this book, you'll learn about all the gear and equipment you'll need to bring on your day or overnight winter outing. Before hitting the trail, check the equipment to make sure it's working properly. Set up your tent and fire up your stove in the back yard. Do a head-to-toe clothing check, verifying that all the people in your group have all their clothing, from hats and sunscreen to socks and boots. Carefully inspect your snowshoes or skis, paying close attention to the straps, clips, and bindings. Review group gear and assign each

Planning Checklist

- ❑ Get comfortable playing in the snow close to home.
- ❑ Enjoy day hikes in your local area.
- ❑ Consider staying in a hut for your first overnight trip.
- ❑ Gather information about backcountry trails by talking with land management agencies, local gear retailers, and outdoor clubs.
- ❑ Purchase maps and update them with your notes.
- ❑ Research the area, including its terrain, weather conditions and potential hazards.
- ❑ Obtain any necessary permits.
- ❑ Winterize your vehicle.
- ❑ Check your gear to make sure it is in good working condition.
- ❑ Give a copy of your itinerary to a friend or family member before setting out.

group member select items to keep in their care and possession throughout the trip.

Never leave home without giving a copy of your itinerary to at least one responsible person who will not be joining you. Itinerary details should include a list of the people in your party, exactly where you will be going, and the alternate routes you might take if hazards arise. You should also note the equipment and clothing you have with you and when you plan to come home. That way, the person knows when and how to initiate a search if you don't return when expected.

Lastly, make sure you know who has the car keys! You won't want to return to your car, exhausted after a long trip, and find that someone forgot them at the last camp. Consider carrying a spare set or hiding keys in a small magnetic box somewhere under the car. If you have your vehicle shuttled, make sure that both you and your driver understand where the keys will be left.

CHAPTER THREE

Groups

For the novice winter traveler, getting started with a group is significantly safer and usually more fun than heading out alone. Group travel and camping brings people together and encourages the development of deep bonds as they share the adventures, laughter, and challenges that highlight every winter wilderness experience. Most often, the weather or snow conditions do not determine whether or not you have a successful outing; how well the group gets along plays a much larger role. As you take more and more trips into the backcountry in winter, you'll develop an appreciation for the importance of choosing companions who share your ambition, fitness level, and definition of acceptable risk.

Assembling the Group

If you were stranded on a desert island and could choose any three people to be there with you, who would you select? Most likely, you would pick the people you trust the most, taking into consideration whether they have skills that could contribute to your survival, well-being, and potential rescue. You would probably want them to have a positive, can-do attitude and a good sense of humor, to boot. The desert island approach works when selecting your winter traveling partners, too. The only problem is that your three most trusted companions may not jump at the opportunity to try winter camping with you. Have no fear—plenty of potential teammates are out there. Your job is to select them wisely.

The most important things to keep in mind when forming a group are individual and group goals and skills, group size, and each person's fitness level, experience, and leadership style. The most effective groups consist of people

With trust and communication, traveling companions can share exhilarating winter experiences.

who willingly contribute their individual skills toward a common goal. The oft-repeated saying that "a group can travel only as fast as its slowest member" applies to the speed of travel, but does not apply in other areas of winter hiking and camping, such as navigation, meal preparation, and decision-making: each individual need not be an expert at everything, as long as at least one person in the group has a skill necessary for a safe, successful trip. One member may be a genius with a map and compass while another excels at cooking and a third sets up super shelters. Trips are most enjoyable when teammates can learn from one another along the way. Just be sure that all the critical skills, such as first aid and navigation, are well represented.

Group Size

Many have debated how large an effective group should be. We're big fans of the number four. Should a group member get injured or ill, one person can attend to that person while the other two look for help. In camp, two can work on building the shelter while the other two set up the kitchen, boil water, and make dinner. A four-person group is also easy to feed—a fairly large one-pot meal will amply serve the group. And a group of this size facilitates travel, as all the participants and their gear can snugly fit in most vehicles.

Some experienced winter hikers choose to enjoy the wilderness on their own, enjoying the peace and solitude that solo trips can offer. This is not recommended for beginners.

Groups larger and smaller than four have their disadvantages. Groups of five or more can be loads of fun, but with more people, potentially conflicting variables—more personalities, needs, desires, and abilities—can create problems. Large groups also put more stress on the environment, exceeding the carrying capacity of the area and destroying the sense of solitude that most winter enthusiasts seek. Small groups of two or three, on the other hand, face increased risk because fewer people are around to contribute their various skills. Small groups are also problematic because someone will have to go alone to find help should an injury occur to another group member.

While four is an ideal number for a group, it isn't always realistic. We often head out—just the two of us—and enjoy very successful winter trips. However, with small groups, you will need to be aware of the increased risk, and you need to take even greater care to avoid problems. The same can be said for solo outings. While we don't encourage heading out alone, we recognize that some very experienced outdoor enthusiasts find winter outings most rewarding when they are completely self-reliant. Should you chose to go solo, make conservative decisions, don't overestimate your abilities, and recognize that you alone are responsible for getting home safely.

Group Goals

Every group, whether it has two people or six, should work together to establish trip goals. Before even choosing a destination or deciding how many hours or days you plan to be outside, ask every group member some simple questions about what they hope to get out of their experience and would like the group to accomplish. Knowing upfront if one person is determined to bag a peak is important, especially if other members of the group would rather search for wildlife or develop their winter camping skills. Review basic group goals, such as working together, maintaining good health, practicing the principles of Leave No Trace, and enjoying the experience, making sure everyone is on board. Be sure that individual and group goals are compatible and flexible.

Leadership

Individual leadership styles often emerge much more quickly—and more dramatically—on winter hiking and camping trips than on other adventures. Factors such as the cold weather and the hard work of hiking through snow add to the pressure the group may feel and could inhibit leaders' abilities to make sound judgments. While strong leadership on a winter expedition is crucial, there is no need for an autocrat to tell the group when to wake up in the morning, how far to travel in a day, what to make for lunch, or when to stop for dinner. Groups function best when leaders consider each member's input and make decisions democratically.

Consultative Leadership

A consultative leadership style is most beneficial when everyone in the group has similar experience and skill sets. Groups organized to run by consensus (which, by our definition, means a "yes" vote from the majority and agreement from everybody to go along with the choice) has both advantages and disadvantages. The advantage is that the consultative process usually results in a full commitment from everybody to group goals and engaged participation in reaching those goals. The disadvantage is that group decision-making takes time (and it isn't always pleasant to stand around in the cold waiting to hear everybody's opinion). If a group chooses to organize this way, it is still crucial that a leader is ready to step in if safety becomes an issue.

Directive Leadership

Some people, especially the young and inexperienced, appreciate a leader who is clearly in charge. A directive leader—usually the person in the group with the most experience and demonstrated ability to make sound judgments—takes much of the responsibility off the group members and saves the group the time required to get everyone's input and reach a consensus. When conditions are severe or if obstacles are between the group and its destination, such as frozen lakes and rivers, a directive leader is the best person to evaluate the situation and figure out the best way to move the group forward.

The most effective leaders demonstrate a wide range of personal and technical skills. They possess strong social skills, along with heightened self- and group-awareness and an ability to tolerate adversity and uncertainty. Leaders must have strong communication skills and, above all, must set a good example by role modeling the behaviors they want to see from other group members. For example, if leaders want group members to layer down after breaks to avoid overheating (before they get sweaty while snowshoeing or skiing), the leaders must be the first to take off their parkas; if they want group members to avoid dehydration, they must drink and urinate throughout the day (and night).

Leaders should also demonstrate compassion. Winter hiking and camping can be intimidating to novices, particularly to young people. When leading others, try to remember your very first outdoor trek—no matter how exhilarating it was, you probably found it scary and unfamiliar. Be patient with inexperienced group members. If you can, offer to carry a little extra gear. Break a little more trail. Help set up shelters. But don't do everything—group members won't learn if they don't have the opportunity to try; they won't buy into group goals if they don't see themselves as contributing members. The biggest danger of a leader trying to do everything for everyone is exhaustion and burnout. Taking care of the group means taking care of all the group members, including yourself.

Jobs on the Trail

One way leaders can keep their energy levels up is by dividing jobs among members. People enjoy taking on responsibilities and receiving recognition for their accomplishments. They take more ownership in their winter hiking and camping experience if they play an active role in making it a success. As part of expedition planning, the group should brainstorm different responsibilities, then determine which roles are necessary for that particular group and divvy them up. Each person in a small group will need to take on more tasks than those in a large group (yet another reason not to hike alone). With some groups, it works best to assign tasks randomly (using such methods as drawing jobs from a hat); with other groups, it's best to ask for volunteers or assign jobs based on members' skill sets. Whichever way you choose, you'll see that

Don't forget to assign the dog a job, too—sometimes the dog is the best trail blazer of the bunch!

everyone gains a sense of commitment to group goals when they can contribute something tangible.

At least one group member needs to take on the role of researching the trip. This position is often filled by the group leader or person who proposed the winter journey. The researcher evaluates the skills and ambitions of individual group members, gathers information concerning trip details (when, where, and how far to go, permits, snow conditions, etc.), and makes final decisions about logistics. The researcher should involve other group members in this process, making sure each person is comfortable with the proposed mileage, route, and terrain. Once the itinerary is decided, the researcher compiles the base map and leaves behind the itinerary with a responsible person who is not going on the trip.

The researcher often takes on the task of handling money, too. Treasurers estimate trip costs, communicate them to other group members, make necessary purchases (or delegate them), record expenses, collect receipts, and act as the banker. If group members lend equipment to the group (or offer a vehicle for transportation to and from the trailhead), the treasurer figures out how to compensate them appropriately.

Another group member should be responsible for the gear and act as equipment manager. Prior to the trip, this person generates a list of personal and group equipment and makes sure that everything is working properly. The equipment manager should also assemble the repair kit (see Chapter 7), depending on what gear the group will take, and needs to make sure that everything on the gear list makes it to the trailhead. During winter camping trips, the equipment manager ensures that all group gear is securely stored in the campsite's "garage" at night (see Chapter 8) and nothing is left behind the following day when setting out from camp.

One of the more enjoyable jobs (in our opinion) is planning the menu. The menu planner solicits meal ideas from the group members and creates a menu that is tasty, varied, and well suited to the physical rigor of the expedition. This person makes sure that often-overlooked things such as spices and oil make the list, then purchases the food and repackages it before the trip. Once on the trail, the menu planner tracks the food supply and makes sure it is appropriately rationed.

Along with the fundamental tasks listed above, others can greatly enhance the group experience, such as by documenting the journey and teaching others about the area's flora and fauna. The naturalist/historian is responsible for researching the region prior to the journey, learning about its human and natural history. This person should carry at least one field guide and often pause on the trail to point out animal tracks or give a mini lesson about winter tree identification or cloud formations. Another person takes the responsibility of bringing a camera and a small group journal, though we usually ask that all members take photos and add journal entries at some point during the trip so that all different perspectives are represented. Each journal entry should at least include the day's time control plan (see Chapter 6) and may also include general comments, stories, poems, drawings, or games. Once we're home, someone usually volunteers to make photocopies of the journal entries and CDs of the photos so that each group member will have a memento.

With so many different tasks, group leaders must be well organized and possess strong communication skills. They need to keep everyone up-to-date about progress during pre-trip planning, make sure all members know what to do, and motivate people to finish their tasks before the group hits the trail. With email and other online tools, keeping each other in the loop during the planning process and asking for help or input whenever needed is easy.

Kids on the Trail

Children can start enjoying winter outings before they even learn to walk, as long as they are bundled up in appropriate clothing (see Chapter 4) and carried in a child carrier or pulled in a sled or trailer. Consult with your family physician to help determine when your child is ready to handle the inevitable bouncing and jostling that comes with traveling in a child carrier or sled. Babies usually have sufficient neck strength after six months.

If you plan to carry your baby or small child in a carrier on your back, note that you won't be able to haul as much of your own gear. Collaborate with another adult to share a pack, and take turns carrying the pack and the carrier. The carrier should fit somewhat like a backpack (see Chapter 5) and have at least one compartment for storing personal gear, such as a water bottle, snack food, and an extra layer or two. After you take a child carrier off your back, always remove the child. Children left unattended in a child carrier are at risk of toppling over, as the carriers are not designed to be freestanding.

Because the risk of falling is greater while skiing than while snowshoeing, we recommend not skiing with a child in a carrier on your back. You wouldn't want to risk hurting yourself and your baby. For skiers, sleds and trailers are better options for transporting children because the child will be much less likely to be injured if the skier falls. Because snowshoers also can use sleds, they are more versatile than child carriers. If you'd like, you can adapt a bike trailer by taking off the wheels and adding ski attachments. When finished, you will have an enclosed ski trailer with great ventilation!

It takes a good deal of effort to carry children in carriers or pull them in sleds or trailers. Adjust your mileage goals accordingly and remain on flat trails or gently rolling terrain. Babies and toddlers will want to stop often to rest, snack, play, drink, and go about their normal daily activities, so plan to take many breaks.

As soon as children express interest in hiking and carrying their own backpacks, they should give it a try. When all members of the family carry their own items, such as food, water, and extra clothing, everyone benefits. Parents' loads become lighter and children have their own emergency gear with them, which will be essential in the unlikely event that they get lost or separated from the group. Small children can use a fanny pack until they're ready for a small daypack. They probably won't wear daypacks for very long, so parents should be prepared to carry them occasionally.

A general rule in summer is that children can travel the same number of miles as their age minus two. For example, 5-year-olds can travel 3 miles in the summer. Now divide that in half for winter travel, as it almost always takes twice as long to reach your destination in the snow. Expect those same 5-year-olds to travel about 1.5 miles on snowshoes or cross-country skis. It might be tempting to go farther than you originally planned if you see your child is doing well and

Children generally love winter hiking because it offers great adventure. Motivate them to keep moving on the trail by pretending an average hike is really an "elk hunt" or a "moose safari." Have them search for animal tracks as they go. Small children enjoy the game "Look for the Alphabet," in which they search for the shapes of various letters in nature. Another popular game with children of all ages is "Twenty Questions." And almost all kids love the opportunity to invent stories, sing songs, and generally act goofy on the trail. During breaks or in camp, kids can build snowmen or create snow angels, but remind them to brush the snow off their clothes once they're finished so that they won't get wet.

having a great time, but avoid that temptation. We've seen many small children have major meltdowns within the last quarter mile from the trailhead. Set your children up for success by starting with very short trips and going slowly. If they have a great experience their first few times hiking in winter, they'll want to go back again and again, and eventually they'll be able and willing to travel greater distances. Before long, you might be the one struggling to keep up!

Personal Responsibility

Whether or not you are a parent or the group leader, your personal contribution is necessary for the group's success. Maintaining a positive attitude is at least 90 percent of what determines a fun, successful outing. This will be much easier to accomplish if you are fit and healthy and keep track of your gear and equipment.

Once, when leading a group of teenagers on a camping trip through Yosemite, we kept falling short of our destination because we had to retrace our steps every few miles to collect a mitten or hat that one young woman left behind at each rest stop. The group was annoyed at the young woman, and she was embarrassed, cold, and increasingly miserable. After backtracking three times to retrieve various articles of clothing, we realized that she had never learned to turn around and make sure she had collected all her belongings before setting off. At home in her urban environment, leaving behind an accessory was not a problem—she could do without it for the few minutes she was outside, or she could easily purchase a replacement. Once she learned the importance of

When all individuals contribute, the group can enjoy incredible experiences, such as reaching the summit of Sunday River Whitecap in the White Mountains.

carefully checking her surroundings and collecting her gear before departing, we were back in business. Group morale was up—as was our mileage—and the young woman felt empowered to keep going.

Even with a positive attitude, good gear, and a high level of fitness and health, winter travel in the wilderness is always going to be at least somewhat risky. Too often, winter adventurers take the availability of rescue for granted, which leads to relaxed planning and a false sense of security. Because rescues are expensive and put rescuers in danger, one of your responsibilities is to do everything you can to minimize the need for outside help. Accepting the freedoms of the wilderness means accepting the responsibility of dealing with any situation that may arise.

One simple way to mitigate your risk is to be mindful of your senses throughout your trip. While stretching your comfort level in order to learn new skills is important, you should listen to your gut when it's telling you to be cautious and to stop and evaluate a situation before venturing forth. Be honest with your group mates about how you feel. Stopping and resting for ten minutes to regain strength or tend to a blister is better than pushing yourself to camp, only to find that you can go no farther because you've pushed yourself too hard.

CHAPTER FOUR
Winter Wear

The first time we led high school students on a winter hiking trip, in 1999, we diligently checked everybody's gear before leaving town. Around the circle, all students held up their long underwear, fleece, parkas, shells, mittens, gaiters, and boots. When Ryan failed to produce a hat, saying he hated wearing anything over his hair, we patiently explained how much heat is lost from one's head. Reluctantly, he accepted a fleece hat from the pile of extra gear. We convinced Austin that yes, he could live without cotton socks, and we even talked Tina into wearing long underwear, although she made us promise never to take her picture in those stinky, unbecoming things. We were feeling good. Our students, we thought, were well equipped for the winter woods.

Unfortunately, we didn't make them try on everything before we hit the trail. Many of the students had borrowed clothing or bought new clothes without making sure they fit properly, especially when layered. After hiking for fifteen minutes, snow started falling, and we asked everyone to rest, put on insulating layers and shells, and drink some water. When only one person could zip her jacket around her parka (the others' jackets were too small), we realized that keeping the group warm and dry would be difficult. We decided to turn around and go home. It was an intelligent choice, given the situation, and we vowed to never put ourselves (or anyone else, for that matter) in the same situation again. On every trip we've subsequently led, we have had participants try on all their gear to make sure that it fits when layered together.

Effective layering requires practice, and finding the right clothes for your personal layering system takes time. All our bodies are built differently. Some people have a hard time cranking up their internal furnaces, while others seem as if they're constantly sweaty. Some people's fingers get cold easily, and others can't keep their toes warm. Before you run out to buy a complete set of technical

Review your basic human thermodynamics (body heat gain versus body heat loss) to understand how to stay comfortable in sub-average temperatures. Your body's metabolic engine, fueled by calories, is your best source of heat. External sources—fire, sun, and chemical hand-warmers—can help you gain heat, but they aren't always available. Exercise is the best way to generate heat in the winter, which is the reason we often instruct students complaining of the cold to get up and do some jumping jacks or take a brisk walk.

Always keep a layer of insulation between your body and the snow, as conduction is one of the four means of human heat loss (along with convection, radiation, and evaporation). Conduction is heat lost through direct contact with a cooler object, such as snow or cold rock. While hiking, conductive heat loss usually occurs when the soles of your boots repeatedly come in contact with snow; while resting, it happens while you're lying or sitting on cold ground. To avoid conductive heat loss when taking a break, lay your backpack on the ground and sit on the part of your pack that wraps around your back. In camp, rest on your closed-cell foam pad. If you're standing for an extended period of time, as you often do while cooking over the stove, place an insulated pad beneath your boots.

winter wear, start paying attention to how your body responds in cold weather. Remember, your body keeps you warm, not your clothes. Clothes merely provide insulation to trap your body's heat.

Layering

As a winter hiker or camper, you'll learn to constantly anticipate the changing conditions and alter your clothing accordingly. Warmth from your body is trapped between your body and the fabric, as well as between separate layers of fabric. This is one reason why wearing several layers of clothing is more effective than one thick layer. Other reasons include the way weather and activity levels change; layering allows you the freedom to shed an article of clothing when either the temperature or your activity level increases. When either of them drops, you can add a layer or two to trap your body heat within your clothing.

You probably already know the basics of a layering system, which is comprised of a protective shell over insulating middle layers over wicking base

To avoid overheating when the temperature is moderate and your activity level is high, shed clothing and wear only your base layers.

layers. If unfamiliar with the layering system, you may think putting all these clothes over each other will make you so bulky that moving will be difficult. Fortunately, most modern outdoor wear is made with some stretch fabric, and most materials have become less cumbersome without sacrificing warmth.

Base layers—including long underwear, liner socks, and liner gloves—provide minimal insulation but effectively wick moisture away from your skin. Insulating middle layers—wool sweaters, fleece pants, and down parkas, for example—trap your warmth and ideally move moisture from your skin. Protective outerwear, such as shells, jackets, and pants, shields you from wind and weather while retaining at least some breathability (see figure 4.1).

Create your layering system with the following goal in mind: the layers you choose should complement each other without being redundant. Take your favorite seven-layer dip, for example: each layer—from refried beans to salsa and from sour cream to cheddar cheese—serves its function, providing substance, flavor, spice, or texture. If you have too many beans, your dip will be chalky and bland, nearly indigestible. Too much sour cream? Yuck. Together and in the right proportions, the ingredients complement each other. So should your clothing.

 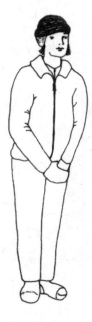 

Base Layers
- Ear band
- Long underwear
- Liner gloves
- Liner socks

Middle Layers
- Warm hat
- Insulating jacket and pants
- Insulating mittens
- Thick wool or synthetic socks

Outerwear
- Sunglasses
- Waterproof jacket
- Bib pants with zippered sides
- Shell mittens
- Gaiters
- Boots

Fig. 4.1. By using proper layering techniques, you'll be able to shed and add clothing as needed.

When you're out in the backcountry and need to take a break from hiking or skiing, add another layer. You may be tempted to cool off first, but avoid that temptation; adding a layer while still warm is the only way to trap your body heat before it inevitably plunges during rest. When you're ready to hit the trail again, remove the layer. You'll be tempted to keep the layer on, but moving while slightly cold is preferable to starting out warm and quickly working yourself into a sweat. Children and teenagers, in particular, have a hard time understanding this counterintuitive concept. Help them.

Clothing Materials

A long time ago, winter adventurers had very few choices when shopping for gear to protect themselves from Mother Nature's elements. Clothing design has

Although they may be cozy when lounging around the house, cheap fleece garments won't be helpful in the outdoors, where seams will easily come apart and the fleece will pill and quickly lose its ability to insulate. Polar fleece (also known as microfleece or micrafleece) clothing sold by outdoor retailers will last much longer and be far more beneficial to you than most fleece clothing found in department stores. Polar fleece garments made specifically for outdoor use have stronger seams and more tightly napped fibers. Be sure to buy polyester fleeces, as they are superior to those made from acrylic material.

improved significantly in recent years, however, with technical advancements in areas such as moisture control (wicking) and temperature regulation. With all the high-tech gear out there, it's easy to get confused about the purpose of each material and its role in your larger layering system. In reality, only three types of materials are acceptable for winter wear: wool, synthetics, and down. Under no circumstances should you take cotton into the elements.

Wool

Wool is a great insulator, as its crimped fibers effectively trap air, even when wet. Wool is woven in varying degrees of thickness and can provide a decent windproof layer when tightly woven. A big advantage is its affordability: wool is often less expensive than other synthetic materials and may be found in the back of your closet. Wool's primary disadvantage is that it becomes heavy when wet and usually dries slowly. It's also bulky, so it requires significant pack room.

Synthetics

Synthetics, such as polypropylene, pile, and polyester, make excellent materials for winter outings. Their ability to insulate is similar to wool. While synthetics dry more quickly than wool, wet wool will keep you warmer than wet synthetics. However, synthetics usually feel more comfortable against your skin, weigh less, and are less bulky. Synthetics provide varying degrees of warmth, depending on the plastic used (polyester traps more heat than polyethylene, which traps more heat than nylon) and the tightness of its weave. This is the reason you will find synthetic materials in base, insulating, and outer layers. Woven very tightly, synthetics can block wind and even keep out precipitation when coated.

Down

Down is the soft, first plumage of certain young birds. Many winter enthusiasts consider down-filled apparel their favorite because it compresses easily and is incredibly warm without being heavy. However, people who wear down must care for it and keep it dry. Once wet, down is practically useless: It easily absorbs water, takes a long time to dry, and loses its ability to insulate. It's also expensive. We never bring down into wet regions, such as the Cascade Mountains. In dry regions, such as the Rockies, we're always happy to have our treasured down vests on hand. If we were high rollers living in a dry climate, we would have full outfits made of down. For now, we're happy with wool and synthetics. You can be, too.

Upper Body Clothing

Protecting your upper body—your heart's home—is the best way to ensure that blood keeps pumping to your legs, fingers, and toes. Start with a base layer against your skin. It should be made from either wool or synthetic materials, which are most effective at wicking moisture away from your body. Personally, we prefer synthetic long-underwear tops to wool ones, since wool feels scratchy and we tend to sweat easily, so it's important for us to use quick-drying fabrics. Many of our friends wear Merino wool because they prefer the feel of natural fiber on their skin, they find wool is less likely to retain odor than synthetic fabrics, and Merino is less scratchy than other types of wool. Regardless of the material you choose, your shirt should include a partial front zipper to aid in ventilation. That will come in handy on dry, sunny winter days when your aerobic level is high and you've stripped down to your base layer. On cooler days—or when your level of activity is lower—you'll want an additional, thicker base layer, often called an expedition-weight layer. This should fit snugly over your long underwear without restricting any movement.

Insulation Layers

The upper body insulation layers—fleece jackets, down vests, wool sweaters, and synthetic parkas, among others—are responsible for trapping the majority of your body's heat. While an overwhelming variety of insulating tops is available, it is most important to find a few that comfortably trap your warmth and complement each other when worn together. When traveling, you will most often be wearing one insulating layer only (if any) over your base layer and you may prefer that it have some ability to resist wind, as many modern fleece layers do. When you stop to rest, you should wear an additional insulating layer

When buying your garments, pay close attention to the location of pockets, zippers, seams, and stretchy fabrics. Make sure zippers have pull-tabs that make them easy to manipulate when wearing mittens. To prevent chaffing beneath pack straps, look for seams that will not lie directly beneath the strap when it rests on top of your shoulders. Be sure pockets are accessible when wearing a pack and ventilation is possible near the parts of your body that perspire most profusely. Experiment with armpit zippers, waist cinches, and cuff closures to see what works for you. Put on all your layers to be sure they fit together.

over everything else. Wearing all layers simultaneously, you may not feel very nimble, but you will feel warm—and that's what matters most when it's time to rest.

Shells

Upper body outerwear garments are often called shells. You can find wind shells, breathable shells, waterproof shells, and even shells that attempt to be all of the above. If you already own one, you should pack a lightweight wind

Waterproof and breathable shell pants and jackets help keep moisture out while allowing ventilation.

shell, because it is compact and will come in handy during aerobic activities. However, wind shells do not block precipitation, and because insulating layers now contain wind-blocking fabrics, this layer can be redundant. Soft shells, on the other hand, can both block wind and repel water, so they offer greater versatility. They breathe well, dry quickly, and are durable and stretchy, but the high price tag reflects this. Be aware that water-repellant shells are not waterproof; soft shells are great when precipitation is minimal or nonexistent, but they do not replace a waterproof shell, which will keep you dry (a key element to keeping you warm). If you can afford the cost and added weight of a soft shell, bring it. If not, bring only a waterproof shell. If the waterproof shell keeps precipitation from seeping through but is not breathable, however, your sweat will stay trapped beneath your shell and you'll get wet anyway. The best shells are waterproof, breathable shells that block weather from penetrating, while allowing perspiration to escape.

Lower Body Clothing

The same principles that apply to upper body clothing also apply to lower body clothing—a good layering system is comprised of shell pants over an insulating layer over a base layer. Fortunately, your lower body doesn't require as much insulation as your upper body, so most people are comfortable with only one insulating layer protecting their lower body, even on the most frigid days.

Underwear

Lower body long underwear should be made from either wool or synthetic materials. Some days you may find the weather warm and dry enough to travel wearing your base layers only, so you'll want long underwear bottoms you will feel comfortable wearing in the company of other trail goers. You won't need to wear briefs or other underwear unless you want to prevent chaffing. If you do opt for additional underwear, be sure it's made of a quick-dry synthetic material. Avoid cotton underwear, as it will defeat the purpose of wearing a base layer, which is designed to keep you dry at skin level.

Insulation Layers

Insulating lower body layers—synthetic or wool pants—should be easy to put on and take off. Pants with full or partial side zippers are best, as they facilitate removal over boots. Some mid-layer pants are gender-specific, offering additional zippers in appropriate places to make urinating easier. Expedition-weight undergarments often suffice as insulating lower body layers.

Shell pants with full side zippers are especially advantageous when your activity level is high and you need some extra ventilation.

Outer Layers

Waterproof and breathable shell pants or bibs with full side zippers are the best lower body outer layers. By keeping your legs warm, your feet will also stay warm and you won't suffer from overall heat loss. We prefer bibs to pants, since bibs rise up the torso and prevent snow and cold air from leaking in around the waist. If you can't afford both waterproof and breathable shells, opt for waterproof ones with side zippers. That way, you can at least open and close the zippers while you're traveling to allow for ventilation. You will have to be more diligent about not overheating, but staying dry will be easier if you can keep weather from getting in.

Clothing for the Extremities

The old saying "If your feet are cold, put on a hat," does hold some merit, as some 70 percent of heat is lost through the head. But hands, feet, toes, fingers, and ears are often the most difficult to keep warm, even if your core is well insulated and your hat wraps snugly around your head. Your heart must work extremely hard to pump blood all the way out to the extremities. Although

You may think the outdoor elements are hard on clothes, but what happens indoors really wears a garment down. As soon as you get home from an outing, lay all your clothing out to dry. Before cleaning anything, double check to see if the item does, in fact, need a cleaning; most insulating and outer layers can withstand multiple uses without a washing, and cleaning garments too often breaks down the fabric. Read the label on every clothing item for its care instructions and follow them carefully. In general, waterproof/breathable shells and down garments should be washed as infrequently as possible; when you do wash them, do so only by hand in cold water with powder detergent (no bleach). Fleece can be laundered regularly, but should always be turned inside out to minimize pilling. Wool garments can either be hand washed or dry cleaned, depending on the manufacturer's recommendations. Wool has a tendency to shrink considerably in warm water, so wash only in cold water. With any outdoor clothing, line drying is preferable to tumble drying in a machine. Mechanical dryers can damage some high-tech garments because forced heat shrinks many different types of fabric and may even melt or warp synthetic garments.

jumping jacks and running in place can help push warm blood to these far-away body parts and warm them, only clothing will effectively trap this heat.

Headwear

We have a thing for headwear, as one of our top priorities is protecting our noggins. Before each trip, we dig into the hat drawer and find the three or four head accessories that best suit the trip we are planning.

For day hikes when the temperature feels warm, we each bring a baseball cap for sun protection and an ear band made of windproof fabric. This keeps our ears warm while allowing excess heat to release through the tops of our heads when we're exercising hard. We also bring a thin hat and a thick hat that are both made of wool or synthetic. We can put one or both of these hats over our ear bands if our heads get cool or when we stop to rest. We always wear our ear bands during aerobic activity and keep our thinner hats in easily accessible pockets. We add and remove this layer at least ten times on an average day hike, as altering headwear is one of the most effective ways to control body heat amid slight temperature or activity changes. As soon as we stop to rest, we pull our heavier hats from our pack and immediately add them over our ear bands and

Glacier glasses with full wrap-around protection are especially valuable when traveling in the sunshine over snow for extended periods.

Goggles keep your face warm and protected and allow you to see, even when wind is whipping snow all around you.

liner hats. We remove the heavier hats after resting and before returning to the trail so that we avoid overheating.

On overnight trips or when we anticipate sub-zero temperatures or wind speeds greater than 20 miles per hour, we bring all of the above and add a scarf and a balaclava to our layering system. A balaclava covers everything from your shoulder blades on up, leaving openings for your mouth, nostrils, and eyes. When we're expecting bitter cold, we bring both an expedition-weight balaclava and a wool or synthetic scarf, which is great at preventing core heat from escaping from the area around the shoulders and neck.

Head accessories include sunglasses, goggles, and face masks. You should always have sunglasses on hand in the winter, as ultraviolet (UV) rays reflect off snow with greater intensity than they do off other surfaces. Snow blindness is a realistic concern in the winter (see Chapter 10) but can easily be avoided if you wear sunglasses that offer full wrap-around protection. When high winds and extreme weather might be a concern, pack ski goggles; they will protect your eyes from debris and make seeing easier. A face mask, like goggles, is only necessary on the coldest of days. Most face masks cover every part of your head and face except for your eyes and mouth and are made of neoprene or a similar material that will not ice up with the condensation from your breath. If you feel your cheeks or nose start to sting from the cold, you'll know it's time to put on your face mask.

Handwear

Trying to do a simple task, such as tying your shoes, when your fingers feel frozen can be extremely frustrating. Wearing layers over your hands—and keeping them dry—is the key to warm fingers. For our hands, we employ the classic layering system. (By now you should have the layering system committed to memory. It is your clothing mantra!) Against our skin, we start with thin synthetic liner gloves. They should be thin enough that you still have finger dexterity for tying knots and clipping buckles and snaps. Some base layer gloves have half fingers that allow for increased finger dexterity. Over those, we layer on insulating mittens, which are warmer than gloves. Each finger acts like a tiny heater, warming the dead air around it, and mittens effectively trap that heated air. Mittens, however, allow for less finger dexterity than gloves. Modular mittens with flip-open tops are a good compromise. A shell mitten—preferably made with waterproof and breathable materials—covers the base and insulating

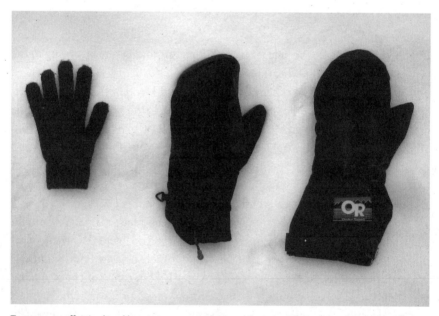

To create an effective hand layering system, wear liner gloves inside insulating mittens inside shell mittens that are waterproof and breathable.

layers. This outer layer is used on only the coldest days, but carrying a pair with you would be wise. You may need only your base gloves to protect your hands on mild winter days or when you're working hard, but you'll always want additional layers. Cold fingers are no fun and may even be permanently damaged if exposed to the elements for too long (see Chapter 10).

Footwear

Happy feet make happy travelers in any season. Whereas keeping your feet cool and blister-free is the obvious concern in the warmer months, during the winter your focus becomes keeping your feet warm and dry.

Socks

Start with a pair of thin liner socks and then add a thicker, warmer wool or synthetic sock over that. If you experience consistently poor circulation to your feet, you may want to consider wearing a vapor-barrier (VB) layer between your thin liner socks and thicker insulating socks. VBs, in general, are materials (typically plastic or coated nylon) that resist the passage of moisture. VB socks—or even plastic bags, secured around your liner socks and feet—prevent perspiration from leaking out, eventually raising the humidity level near the skin so that sweating slows or even stops. If you are interested in wearing a VB layer, we recommend experimenting with plastic bags before you throw down plastic credit cards on a purchase; getting comfortable using VB takes some time and not everyone is a fan.

Keeping Socks Dry

Always keep at least one pair of socks dry. On a day hike, keep the spare pair in a Ziploc bag. On an overnight or multiday trip, bring one or two additional pairs and always keep one of those pairs in the bottom of your sleeping bag when you're not wearing them during the night. If a pair gets wet, dry them by placing one sock directly on each thigh, between your skin and your base layer. It may seem a little odd, but your body is your best heat source and your thighs will warm and dry your socks in just a few hours. You could also use this method to dry wet gloves or hats. If you do go this route, you can use more than your thighs at your human heat source—try your armpits or your belly.

Boots

Winter boots come in a variety of styles, but all good ones share at least a few characteristics: they are insulated, made to accommodate thicker socks, and have a thick sole and good tread. Beyond that, you need to find the boot that fits your foot best and is best suited to the conditions and sport you plan to pursue. Unless you're a pro at keeping your feet dry, you should wear a waterproof boot. As in other seasons, make sure you have your boots fitted correctly and then break them in around town before you hit the trail. The following is a list of common winter boots and their uses:

Insulated or pack boots. These boots are great for extreme cold and fit well with snowshoes. They have thick rubber bottoms, leather or synthetic waterproof uppers, and removable liners, which are usually made from dense wool felt. However, an increasing number of manufacturers are producing pack boots with synthetic liners, which is good news for sweaty feet. If your boots do come with wool felt liners, you can always replace them with synthetic ones. A disadvantage of pack boots is their tendency to retain a significant amount of heat, which could cause your feet to get sweaty and wet. They also

Caring for Your Boots

Be good to your boots. Depending on the style of boots you choose to wear in the winter—leather boots, ski boots, mouse boots, snowboard boots, or mountaineering boots—they may need to be treated before you hit the trail. Leather boots, in particular, require a healthy dose of preventative care. Waterproof them before you wear them outside for the first time, following the manufacturer's instructions. The less water absorbed by leather, the longer it will last and the more comfortable it will be. Once you start using any kind of boot in the elements, you'll notice that it reacts similarly to skin when exposed to sun, snow, water, and wind—it becomes brittle. After each trip, clean your boots with a dry cloth and, if necessary, with water and a nylon brush (for leather). If your boots have removable liners, take them out and let them dry completely. If the boot liners aren't removable, stuff wads of newspaper in the toes of the boots to absorb moisture, then replace wet newspaper with dry newspaper, and repeat until the boot is moisture-free. Only after the boots are completely dry should they be stored. Ski boots should be put away buckled, with their liner folds properly in place in order to retain their shape and comfort.

fit more loosely than stiffer boots, which could cause discomfort for those wanting greater support. Pack boots are the most common and versatile of the winter boots. If you plan to wear them with snowshoes, make sure the two fit together.

Ski touring boots. These specialized cross-country skiing boots offer insulation, support, breathability, and water resistance. They are also flexible enough to allow for the kick-and-glide motions of cross-country. Modern ski touring boots are made with synthetic materials and many have additional ankle support.

Mountaineering boots. Otherwise known as hard-core double boots, these consist of rigid outer boots—often made of plastic—and inner boots made with synthetic materials assembled into open- or closed-cell foam. As the name suggests, these boots are made for mountaineering; the rigid outer boot performs well in challenging terrain and the inner boot retains body heat and dries quickly. However, these boots can be heavy and awkward to walk in and are expensive.

Mukluks. These are just about as far from mountaineering boots as can be, yet many people still find them to be comfortable for many winter outings—as

Mountaineering boots made with hard plastic and crampons perform well in challenging terrain.

Camp booties are the luxury footwear of winter camping.

Gaiters keep snow from entering in through the top of your boots and soaking your feet.

long as they stay dry and their lack of ankle support is not a major concern. Mukluks are one-piece moccasins that rise almost to the knee and have thick wool felt linings that are usually removable. They are flexible and breathable, offering comfort but not much support. However, they can only be worn when the snow is dry and powdery, as they are not waterproof.

Camp booties. Perhaps more similar to slippers than boots, these are indispensable for keeping your feet warm in the tent or around camp in dry conditions. Camp booties are filled with synthetic fiber or down and most have hard soles for walking around and draw-cord cuffs to retain warmth.

Mouse boots. If you're looking for a cost-effective alternative to expensive pack boots or mountaineering boots, or if you're trying to outfit a group of young people, opt for mouse boots. These boots, also known as Mickey Mouse or bunny boots, were first issued to GIs during the Korean War and were designed to protect soldiers from water and extreme cold. They have a wool-lined interior and several layers of rubber to serve as insulation. They do, in fact, look like Mickey Mouse's boots, and their thick soles help prevent conductive heat loss. They're widely available online and at army surplus stores for an affordable price. Their disadvantage is their weight, bulk, and inability to breathe. But if the choice is between these and your warm-weather hiking boots, choose these.

- ❑ Liner hat
- ❑ Fleece ski hat
- ❑ Balaclava
- ❑ Sunglasses
- ❑ Goggles
- ❑ Lightweight long underwear top
- ❑ Midweight long underwear top
- ❑ Pile sweater
- ❑ Pile vest
- ❑ Waterproof/breathable shell jacket
- ❑ Liner gloves
- ❑ Insulating gloves or mittens
- ❑ Shell mittens
- ❑ Lightweight long underwear pants
- ❑ Fleece pants with full side zippers
- ❑ Waterproof/breathable pants or bibs
- ❑ Liner socks (2 pair)
- ❑ Wool socks (3 pair)
- ❑ Gaiters
- ❑ Boots
- ❑ Camp booties

Gaiters. Layering applies to the feet in much the same way that it does to other parts of the body. Over your socks and boots, layer protective shells, called gaiters. These strap under the arch of your hiking boots, wrap around your ankles and calves, and prevent snow from getting into your boots at your ankles. At the very least, get gaiters that are water resistant, but waterproof and breathable gaiters are much better options. If you are expecting sub-zero temperatures, chose expedition-weight gaiters that have some insulation.

Kids' Clothing

Babies, toddlers, and small children require the most protection from the elements, as they can become overheated or hypothermic quickly and usually can't tell you how they're feeling or ask for your help. Because they often sit in a child carrier or sled, they're not exerting as much energy and are at greater risk of getting cold. Layer them in clothing similar to that which you are wearing. For babies, one-piece, footed pajamas make good base layers, as long as they are not cotton. Babies' diapers need to be checked and changed frequently, as moisture next to the skin can contribute to hypothermia. Regularly check children's hands and feet and the back of their necks to gauge their temperature. Lastly, make sure children have proper sun protection.

Traveling Light

Ultra-light hiking and backpacking is all the rage these days, and it makes us downright uneasy. Sure, very experienced outdoors people have had much success paring down their clothing, food, and gear during warm-weather adventures, but dropping weight in the winter is not nearly as critical as having what you need when you need it to stay warm and dry. A basic layering system of clothing for every part of your body—from your feet to your head to your hands—is essential to your survival. At the same time, lugging around excess weight (unnecessary, redundant layers or extra sets of clean clothes) will make it more difficult to travel, which also puts you in danger. Carry what you need. No more. No less.

CHAPTER FIVE
Traveling Gear

The first few times Yemaya ventured onto the trails in winter more than 15 years ago, she was faced with the classic debate over whether to rent snowshoes or cross-country skis. She owned neither, had no real winter hiking skills to speak of, and lacked the money needed to buy the finest equipment and instruction. So, logically, she chose snowshoes for their affordability and ease of use. After renting different snowshoes for a year or so and graduating from groomed trails to unbroken backcountry, she invested in the shoes she liked best and then happily hit the trails every chance she had.

Lucas grew up wearing snowshoes throughout the winter, so by the time he and Yemaya met, he had already started to envy the cross-country skiers he saw on backcountry trails. They seemed to glide by effortlessly, floating atop the very snow we were trudging through with our clunky snowshoes. Back at the gear shop, we both rented cross-country skis and boots, and soon invested in pairs of our own. We could go farther—faster!—and within a few trips we could even take turns and descend slopes without falling flat on our faces. Life was grand. But then the mountains called.

We noticed all the telemark and alpine touring skiers could reach higher places than we could, and we wanted to join them. We spent a long time researching alpine touring skis, and an even longer time saving for the big investment. Once we finally purchased our fat, fancy skis, a whole new world of backcountry terrain spread open before us—what a treat! We could skin up steep slopes, check out spectacular views from high mountain peaks, then lock down our heels and shred turns all the way down to our car.

These days when we head out for a day trip, we often pack the car with all our gear, and wait until we hit the trailhead to see the snow conditions and decide whether we'll strap on the snowshoes or skis. When planning overnight trips or summit attempts, we usually go for the ski-shoe trip, alternating using snowshoes and skis on our ascents (depending on the conditions and terrain) then relying solely on skis for fun, quick descents. We find this to be sublime. The cold, white, snowy landscape is finally part of our world, and we can explore it from sea to summit without sacrificing great comfort. Of course, we're able to enjoy these more advanced expeditions only because we started simple and tried different gear as we developed our skills. We wouldn't have reached this level any other way, and we hope that you, too, start small and acquire new gear only as you need it and know how to use it.

Snowshoes

Since humans first noticed the way snowshoe hares quickly maneuver through deep snow on their oversized feet, we have attempted to emulate nature by creating long, webbed footwear that mimics the properties of hares' hind feet. Snowshoes most likely originated some 4,000 to 5,000 years ago in central Asia, where people attached flat surfaces of leather or round wooden planks to their feet. With the advent of snowshoes, human life changed forever—our territory expanded, and we could travel and hunt in areas previously unexplored.

Today, snowshoeing is one of the fastest growing winter sports in the world and it's easy to understand why: the sport is relatively inexpensive, easy to learn, poses little risk of injury, and is a great way to access backcountry areas that would otherwise be too steep or technical to reach. For beginning winter adventurers, snowshoeing is the way to go. Hiking in snowshoes is far more intuitive than skiing (you'll fall less often), and the old saying generally holds true that "If you can walk, you can snowshoe." Another benefit of snowshoes is their affordability when compared to skis. They are easier to handle over steep terrain and on narrow, serpentine trails. They weigh less than skis, make better impromptu shovels, and usually grip the snow better than their slick competitors.

Snowshoes have operated under the same principle since their inception; they distribute weight over a large area, allowing a person to hike through snow without sinking in. In the past few decades, though, manufacturers have transitioned from "traditional" wood frame "racket style" shoes with rawhide decking to "modern" shoes made of metal or plastic frames with synthetic bindings. Some winter enthusiasts still swear by traditional wood models because they prefer wood's flexibility and the shoe's overall aesthetic appeal. However, an increasing number of hikers find metal and hard plastic models superior; they're incredibly lightweight with unparalleled strength and durability.

Types of Snowshoes

When you start shopping for snowshoes, you'll notice great discrepancy between the least and most expensive pairs. That's because three types of snowshoes are available: recreational/hiking snowshoes, aerobic/fitness snowshoes, and hiking/backpacking snowshoes. Different manufacturers use different materials and offer different features, which determine a particular snowshoe's cost and durability.

Recreational snowshoes. These are the most basic shoes and are great for beginners and casual snowshoers on day hikes. They are the most common snowshoes on the market and while they all share the same basic parts, outfitters offer an amazing variety of them. Some shoes have rounded ends (better for flotation) while others are tapered (allowing for a more natural gait). Some have bindings that wrap around the boots like intricate webs, while others bind simply with a few rubber straps. All recreational snowshoes share the same general structure—bindings attached to decking attached to (and spread tautly across) a frame. While most recreational snowshoes have some sort of cleat beneath the foot's pivot point, the gripping power of recreational snowshoes is not nearly as effective as that of more substantial hiking/backpacking snowshoes. For primarily that reason, recreational snowshoes work

Hiking/backpacking snowshoes are extremely durable. Their solid frames, bindings, decking, and toothed cleats can handle tough backcountry terrain and stay afloat over deep powder.

best on flat, even terrain or on gentle slopes with well-packed snow. They are not conducive to extensive backcountry expeditions when wearing a heavy pack, traveling up steep, uneven terrain, or breaking trail through deep snow. If you are bringing kids along, some manufacturers produce recreational snowshoes for children who weigh up to 90 pounds, including their packs. These shoes are acceptable for short, easy hikes but should not be taken into the backcountry. (For backcountry trips, children should opt for small adult hiking/backpacking snowshoes.)

Aerobic/fitness snowshoes. These are designed for runners and cross-trainers wanting to move quickly over well-packed (often groomed) trails. They have a sleek, narrow design with sharply tapered tails and two-thirds of the weight of other types of snowshoes. Again, they are not suitable for extended trips in the backcountry when wearing a heavy pack.

Hiking/backpacking snowshoes. These snowshoes are built to handle the toughest backcountry terrain and withstand the weight of the heaviest packs. From their solid frame to their bomber bindings and beefy decking, these snowshoes will last for many years. They're great for both deep powder and with their large toothed cleats perform well in icy conditions. Of course, what you gain in strength and durability, you lose in price and weight; these shoes are expensive and heavy. They can be used for other activities, such as recreational or aerobic ones, while recreational and aerobic shoes should not be used for extended backcountry trips.

Even after you've settled on a type of snowshoe, you still need to make number of decisions about frame, decking (webbing), and binding materials. As mentioned above, some snowshoe enthusiasts find traditional wooden frames best. These folks swear by the *feel* of the wood—the organic liveliness that no metal or hard plastic can rival. But even some of the biggest traditionalists can't help but agree that modern snowshoes are the way to go in the backcountry. Most modern shoes are comprised of lightweight aluminum frames, but some popular new models use no metal at all; they're made completely from hard plastic and include detachable tail extenders that can be added or removed depending on the depth of the snow. In our opinion, these offer the most flexibility and highest performance.

Decking

Decking, webbing, and lacing are all words used to describe the material attached to the snowshoe frame that disperses a person's weight over the snow. Snowshoe bindings vary from model to model. Webbing on wooden snowshoes was originally created with strips of rawhide or sinew from beaver, bear, moose, or caribou hide that needed to be treated annually with waterproof varnish. Today, snowshoe manufacturers use either rubber-coated nylon or solid plastic. These materials differ slightly in the way they grip snow and resist wear and tear. Some new snowshoe models have additional decking heel-lifters, called ascenders, that can be raised to facilitate climbing.

Bindings

Whether you've decided to acquire a recreational snowshoe, an aerobic snowshoe, or a backcountry snowshoe, your binding should securely hold your boot in place and prevent your heel from shifting laterally. Bindings are perhaps the element that most determines your satisfaction with your snowshoes. If they can't stay on your feet, they're no good! Bindings come in two styles: limited rotation and free rotation.

Limited rotation shoes lift the tail up with your foot and do not allow the toe to go below the decking. This style of binding is common on aerobic snowshoes and is preferred by anyone wishing to travel quickly, as the tail does not drag with these shoes. They're also good for traveling over downed trees and other obstacles that could get caught in dragging tails. The downside to this style of shoe is how it flips snow up on your backside with each step.

Free rotation shoes do not lift the tail with your foot and do allow the toe to go below the decking. This style of binding is preferred on backpacking snowshoes and by climbers wanting to kick in steps and get traction on steep slopes. Although these shoes don't flip snow up across your back, their free tails are more susceptible to entanglement with downed trees or branches when the snowshoer is traveling through densely forested areas.

Either style of binding should be made from durable materials, such as rubber or thickly coated nylon, that won't freeze. Look for strap buckles that can be easily manipulated with gloved hands, such as those that work on thumb release. Some binding styles incorporate a cup in which to insert the toe, but most have only a series of three straps that are secured around the boot once it's correctly centered on the shoe.

Cleats

Look for snowshoes with strong cleats to provide traction. In general, the larger the cleats, the stronger the grip. You'll want a lateral bar of cleats that runs beneath your toes, as well as teeth that run alongside the frame to facilitate lateral traction. Modern cleats are usually made with either stainless steel (which is heavier) or aluminum (which ices up more frequently). The best models also incorporate a de-icing pad beneath the toe cleat, which helps prevent annoying ice balls from forming and throwing you off balance.

Once you've determined your correct type and style of snowshoe and what materials you want, it's time to select your size. Larger people need larger snowshoes if they expect to stay afloat; smaller people benefit from smaller shoes because they are lighter and easier to maneuver. Snowshoes' weight does matter, as each additional pound on your feet is additional weight your body has to haul around. Smaller shoes are more agile and better for maneuvering through forest obstacles, while bigger shoes offer more flotation and do best in deep, heavy snow. Look at the manufacturer's guidelines to determine what size shoe you need and then consider what snow conditions you anticipate encountering. A common formula states that for every pound of body weight, there should be one square inch of snowshoe surface per snowshoe. In this formula, people should consider their body weight to be their actual body weight plus everything they plan to carry (including their pack, boots, gear, and clothing). For example, if you weigh 180 pounds and the snowshoe you are considering is rated for 200 pounds, make sure additional gear and clothing won't exceed 20 pounds.

Some snowshoe manufacturers make different styles for men and women to accommodate for the anatomical differences between bodies. Because women tend to be lighter than men, women-specific snowshoes tend to be smaller. They are usually tapered because women generally have a narrower stride than men (due to their knees and legs being closer together). The tapered design allows the snowshoes to clear each other while women are hiking with a natural stride. If you are a woman, consider trying female-specific snowshoes to see if you prefer them to unisex models.

Because snowshoes are relatively inexpensive to rent, we recommend you try as many pairs as possible before purchasing the particular style and size that's right for you. It's important that you bring along the boots you plan to wear snowshoeing when you go to rent or purchase so that you can be sure the binding fits those boots. Unless you live to run in snowshoes, getting a pair of recreational or backpacking snowshoes will offer you the most versatility and enjoyment.

Skis

Once you get the hang of it, skiing is the most enjoyable way to access the winter woods. Instead of trudging through snow, skis allow you to glide over it, making it easier to go more places more quickly without expending as much energy. The challenge is that skiing has a steep learning curve (literally) and you may fall a lot when learning. While it takes a bit of practice to get those boards strapped to your feet to go where you want them to go, the rewards are well worth the effort.

As with snowshoes, there are a few different styles of skis to choose from, including cross-country (Nordic) skis, telemark skis, and alpine touring (randonnée) skis. The one thing all these skis have in common that differentiates them from alpine (downhill) skis is that they keep a skier's heels free at least during the ascent to allow a natural hiking motion.

Cross-country skis are favored by traditional adventurers and celebrated by Nordic racers around the globe. Their design is thin, long, and light, making them very fast on flat terrain. Accompanied by lightweight bindings and soft-to-semi-rigid boots, these skinny skis work best on groomed terrain and some easy backcountry trails. Because the heel is not bound to the ski, cross-country skiers perform best over flat or gently rolling terrain in which they're constantly transitioning between ascents and descents. But don't bother with skinny skis on moderate to difficult ungroomed terrain where you'll need skis capable of breaking trail, beefy bindings that will lock down during descents for great control, and boots warm and waterproof.

Long, thin cross-country skis are light and fast over gentle, easy terrain.

Because backcountry conditions are constantly changing, you'll need skis that can adapt. Unlike groomed trails where terrain and snow conditions stay relatively consistent over multiple miles, the backcountry is not manicured and you can't expect current conditions to stay the same for long. Deep, fluffy powder can transition to firm, icy snow or wet slush in just a few hundred feet. You may enjoy following tracks for a mile, then have to slog ahead breaking trail on your own. You need to be ready for anything in the backcountry, so you'll want skis versatile enough to handle a wide range of conditions.

Wide touring skis float well over the snow, making them ideal for ungroomed trails and deep powder.

In our experience, more and more people are choosing shorter, wider touring skis these days that float better over deep snow and offer greater all-around versatility. Skis in the touring category are fat (approximately 80–90mm) and heavy (around 5 or 6 pounds per pair) compared to cross-country skis (which range between 15 and 40mm wide and weigh just a few pounds). They float better over deep snow and are easier to control when going downhill. Here are some questions to ask yourself when evaluating different pairs of touring skis:

How much sidecut should I get? Skis are wider at their tip and tail than in the middle; the difference is called the sidecut. Skis with a deeper sidecut turn faster, while skis with a minimal sidecut maintain their bearing better on flat terrain. Consider your experience level and the terrain you expect to encounter when deciding how much sidecut you want. In general, a moderate cut is good for most beginning and intermediate skiers.

Should I get waxable or waxless skis? Some skis require wax and others substitute plastic bottoms with fish scale patterns. Waxable skis are faster and grip better, provided you've appropriately waxed the skis for the current conditions (which is harder than it looks). Waxless skis are less of a hassle, but they do sacrifice a little bit of glide and traction. If you're one of those gear heads who loves to tinker and don't mind carrying a wax kit, go for the wax. If you're like us, though, stick with the simple fish scale pattern—less time fiddling with your skis means more time shreddin' it on the slopes.

How flexible should my skis be? Touring skis are much more flexible than the ones you wear in the lift line, allowing you to float on deep snow without burying your tips. For mixed conditions, look for a ski with a medium flex to handle a wide variety of snow conditions. Many modern touring skis come with metal edges, which do slightly decrease the skis' flexibility but are infinitely advantageous for their durability and gripping power on crusted snow and ice.

Telemark and alpine touring (randonnée) skis combine the best of what Nordic, touring, and downhill skis have to offer: they travel quickly over flat terrain, scale the steep slopes with competence, then allow for steep descents with speed, control, and agility. The distinction between telemark and randonnée skis decreases day by day as the equipment evolves. The primary difference between the two is that telemark skiing is free-heeled all the time, while randonnée skiing is free-heeled on the ascent only. Telemark ski descents are done using the telemark turn—a technical turn in which the skis are staggered but parallel—and randonnée descents (which mimic alpine ski descents) are made after locking down the boots' heels to the skis' bindings. "Tele" skiers

On his early spring Mount St. Helens climb in the Cascade Range, this hiker employs randonnée skis.

Split Boards

If you're accustomed to carving powder on a snowboard, consider a split board for backcountry travel. Split snowboards are designed to separate into skis for backcountry ascents, then hook back together to form a snowboard when you're ready to pursue boarding's biggest game: deep, uncarved powder. Compared to snowboards, split boards are relatively long and narrow with a deeper sidecut. Special binding hardware allows you to rotate from ride-mode to forward-pointing ski-mode, and most snowboard boots fit perfectly well with these modified boards. Wide climbing skins and specialty crampons are manufactured especially for these boards, allowing you to scale steep pitches. Although split boards were introduced to the market within the last ten years, their ability to perform well within the entire range of backcountry snow conditions—coupled with snowboarding's overall popularity—suggests split boards are not a passing fad.

espouse telemark skiing over randonnée skiing because it's more aesthetically pleasing (the "tele" turn *is* beautiful), more challenging, a better workout, and the skis are generally lighter. Randonnée enthusiasts point out that their gear functions just as well as telemark gear, while being much easier to learn to use, especially if you're already adept at downhill skiing. For you, the choice will come down to personal preference and prior experience. Randonnée skiing is generally better for beginners.

Like a snowshoe, a touring ski is only as functional as its binding. Telemark skis traditionally used a three-pin binding system. Today, they are more likely to have beefier cable bindings more appropriate for backcountry travel in deep snow on steep terrain. Both types of bindings keep your heel entirely free, and new models feature free-hinging heel pieces when the binding is set in touring mode. The feature facilitates climbing and saves you energy and strain when skinning up steep slopes. Randonnée bindings always have two positions—one with the heel free for uphill climbs and one with the heel locked in place for downhill skiing. When in ascending mode, select one of the multiposition heel lifters to ease calf strain. For those traveling in avalanche-prone terrain, be sure bindings do not have safety straps that could impede your ability to release your skis. And whether you choose tele or randonnée bindings, be sure they are compatible with your boots, and work with a respected gear retailer to get the correct fit.

Ski Length

Gear retailers can also help you select appropriate ski length, which is based on your weight, skills, and the particular ski model. In general, longer skis are advantageous if you plan to ski fast on steep slopes; they'll be a little more stable and provide more control. If you plan to spend the majority of your time on variable terrain with backcountry obstacles, such as boulders and tight trees, choose shorter skis. They're more maneuverable and turn more quickly.

Skins

Armed with skis, boots, and bindings, you've nearly outfitted yourself with a complete backcountry ski set—but you still need skins. Skins are textured strips of fabric that adhere to the bottom of skis to provide traction. The name originates from the animal skins that traditional adventurers attached to their skis. With hairs pointed toward the skis' tails, skins allowed skiers to glide forward, but not back. Today's skins are made with synthetic materials, but the principle remains the same. To use skins, simply stick them to the bottom of skis for ascents, then peel them off and pack them away when you're ready to carve turns down powder runs so that the bottom of your skis are slick and free from any friction the skins may provide.

When temporarily adhered to the bottom of skis, skins allow skiers to glide forward, not back.

Allow skins to dry in the sun before taking them off of skis and packing them away.

After you've skied to the top of the slope, you'll want to take a break, enjoy the view, relish in your accomplishment, and sip some water. This is a great time to stick your skis upright in the snow and allow the skins to dry in the sun before packing them away. By drying them immediately, you reduce their risk of becoming moldy in your pack. Drier skins are also lighter than wet ones, which will make your pack lighter for the descent. Once the skins are relatively dry, remove them from the bottom of your skis, carefully fold them into their carrying case, and pack them away until you get home, when you can hang them to dry fully.

Poles and Avalanche Probes

Ever since the days of hunters and gatherers, Homo sapiens have been using walking sticks to improve balance and diminish strain on legs and joints. While good old wooden sticks can serve you well in a pinch, it's worth investing in modern hiking poles. Hiking poles have exploded in popularity in recent years—and with good reason. Anyone with knee or joint pain (and those wishing to avoid such agony in the future) can attest to the benefits of hiking poles. Along with enhancing balance, easing the pack's weight from your shoulders, and decreasing the pressure on your legs and joints, poles also serve as lightweight do-it-all gear items that can help when pitching a tent or tarp. Should the situation arise, they can also be used as avalanche probes and even makeshift splints for broken bones.

In winter, poles are especially recommended. Traveling over snow is generally more taxing on the body than traveling over bare ground, hikers carry more weight in winter than in summer, and the consequences of getting hurt during the winter can be more severe. Poles will help you avoid injury by aiding your balance, which is especially important when you have foreign objects on your feet, such as skis, snowshoes, or crampons. Snow and ice are slippery, too, and poles will help keep your feet beneath you.

If you already have fixed-length ski poles that are long enough, they should suffice even when you're not skiing. To check the fit, turn the poles upside down and grasp them right above their baskets; your upper and lower arm should make a 90 degree angle at your elbow. You'll want to be able to adjust the poles for steep inclines, which is obviously difficult with a fixed-length pole. You can get around this by wrapping duct tape thickly around the pole at a lower grip

Hikers ascending the flanks of Mount Rainier use hiking poles to help maintain balance and form.

point before hitting the trail. (Usually that tape will be handy for other uses at some point in your trip.)

Investing in adjustable poles with at least one or two moveable sections is worthwhile so that you can lengthen the poles on flat and descending terrain and shorten them on steep ascents. These poles are often called telescoping poles. They are made with comfortable and secure hand straps, as well as removable baskets that you can remove for hiking during the other three seasons. Adjustable poles break down nicely and can easily fit under the compression straps of your pack. The best-constructed ones are made with very lightweight carbon fiber and some are incorporated with springs for shock absorption. These poles can function as avalanche probes when necessary.

If you know you will be venturing into avalanche terrain, you should carry actual avalanche probes. They are preferable to telescoping poles because they are designed for one function—to quickly dig through deep snow and reach a buried person. Avalanche probes burrow through snow layers more efficiently and reach almost twice as far. They are also very lightweight and break down into easily storable segments that quickly come together with shock cord. Of course, if you're traveling in avalanche-prone areas and plan to carry probes, you should know how to use them in conjunction with an avalanche beacon. Take an avalanche course and be prepared (see Chapter 10).

The Pack

Backpacks these days are so cool. They come in all different sizes, colors, and designs, and different backpacks are available for every sport imaginable. It can be overwhelming, but here's the good news: if you have a backpack you love using in the summer, you'll most likely love using it in the winter, too—as long as its capacity is large enough to hold the additional gear and clothing you need in the colder months. As your experience level increases, you'll probably find yourself fine-tuning your idea of the ideal winter pack, with its sport-specific features and perfectly situated pockets. Until you're ready to invest in a new pack, enjoy the one you have. But if you're still using that relic of an external frame pack you bought for junior high scout camp, it's time to embrace the internal frame. Because internal frame packs have a lower center of gravity, they carry weight closer to the body, which increases comfort and helps improve balance for those traveling over uneven terrain on skis or snowshoes. These packs also tend to have greater capacity and fewer external straps that tempt you to do something silly (and potentially dangerous) like strap your sleeping bag to the outside of your pack.

When you're ready to invest in a new winter pack, keep a few general guidelines in mind. First and foremost, your pack's capacity needs to be large enough to carry your food, water, clothing and equipment. It should be comfortable and stable, a seemingly natural extension of your body. It must be durable enough to withstand harsh winter conditions in the backcountry. Finally, it should have the added features you need, such as loops and straps for securing an ice ax and skis. Your answers to the questions on the following pages will help you determine which pack best suits your needs:

Are you looking for a pack to take on short aerobic exercises, on day hikes, or on extended backpacking trips? For short aerobic exercises when you're close to a trailhead and don't expect to be out for more than a few hours, you can afford to go light. A small hydration pack or day pack should be sufficient, as long as it can hold a little extra food, water, and clothing. You will need a pack that can hold all that plus some emergency gear (such as a first-aid kit and small sleeping bag) if you plan to be out for four to twelve hours. This is especially important if you will be traveling more than an hour away from a trailhead or will be hiking in challenging conditions. A pack between 1,500 cubic inches and 3,000 cubic inches (roughly 24 to 50 liters) should suffice. For backcountry trips longer than a day or two, you'll want a pack with a capacity of 5,000 cubic inches or greater in order to carry everything from your tent and cookware to additional clothing layers and lots of food. We tend to opt for a pack that is a littler larger;

For short day hikes and aerobic workouts in the wintry outdoors, a small day pack such as this one should suffice.

a larger pack can always be condensed, as long as it has sufficient compression straps. Making a small pack larger is impossible, and you don't want to run the risk of leaving important things at home because they don't fit.

Do you prefer that your pack be more comfortable or that it weigh less? The answer to this question will help you choose the suspension system—the shoulder straps, hip belt, and the internal back pad, stays, or frame sheet—that best suits your desired comfort level. (Usually, packs with the most comfortable suspensions systems and beefiest hip belts and shoulder straps weigh more than those without.) These considerations may not be as obvious to you as the pack's external pockets and design elements, so be careful to not overlook them when shopping for a pack. The suspension system dictates the pack's comfort, and comfort is far more necessary than cool features.

Since you'll be carrying the majority of the weight on your hips, make sure the hip belt rides comfortably and is adjustable. Shoulder straps, which stabilize and support your load, should also be adjustable so that you can move the pack away from or closer to your shoulders as you wish. A sternum strap will also help stabilize the load and keep it close to your body so that the pack turns and twists with you. Look for compression side straps that keep the load secure, bringing it snug to your back. Compression straps will squeeze down your pack as its load diminishes (when you eat food or go for a shorter trip than usual) and can be used to secure skis and poles. The last aspect of the suspension system to consider (but perhaps the most important) is the internal frame. A knowledgeable gear retailer will be able to help you find a pack that best fits your torso.

Is there a particular winter sport (such as skiing) that you plan on doing most when using this pack? This will help you decide the pack features you need. People with the cash and commitment to buy the best bag on the market are often impressed by all the bells and whistles of modern packs. While the added pockets, zippered panels, and quick-release straps allow for better organization, they also increase a pack's weight and potentially decrease its functionality. External pockets could make it difficult to attach skis and other equipment to your pack. Additional straps, clips, and zippers have a greater likelihood of freezing, breaking, or getting caught up on downed trees in the winter, when you're often scrambling over them. We're big proponents of simple, large top-loading packs with just a few features, including the following:

- *A lid pocket.* This is a great storage space for items you will want to access quickly, such as a map, compass, light source, and extra hat.
- *A side zipper.* It provides access to the pack's main compartment for reaching clothes or food without having to dig through your pack.
- *One or two ice ax loops.* These are most effective when their ax attachment strap has a quick-release buckle. Ice ax loops are standard on most backcountry packs, but quick-release buckles are not. With gloved hands, they're essential.
- *Side compression straps with quick-release buckles.* These features are great for stabilizing the load, as well as securing skis or poles to the pack for quick access.

There is usually more than one pack that will fit your needs and include features you want. Try on as many packs as you can before making a purchase. Just think—a pack carries *everything* you need in the backcountry. It's going to be heavy, so it better be comfortable.

Fitting a Pack

Fitting a pack correctly is an art form. We can't tell you how many times we've helped both children and adults on the trail by merely adjusting their packs. Whenever we hear people complain about their terrible packs and painful shoulders, we immediately look at the way their packs fit; it's usually not pretty. More often than not, the pack size is correct for the person's torso, but the person has no idea how to utilize the suspension system to situate their load correctly. We tug a little here, release a little there, and after redistributing the weight, the hiker usually looks at us as if we've just turned water to gold. To avoid the pain in the first place, keep some tricks in mind from the moment you try on a pack in the store to your fifth mile on the trail.

Ask a knowledgeable gear retailer to help you choose a pack that is the correct size for your torso, which you'll want to measure by running a measuring tape from the pronounced bone at the base of your neck down the middle of your back to the level of your hip bones. Many manufacturers create different packs for men, women, and children. You'll want to find the one that corresponds to your body type. Before trying a pack on, try your best to simulate a backcountry experience. Wear everything you would wear in the most challenging conditions you expect to face. Pack the pack with everything you plan to carry on the longest trip you anticipate taking. You can either bring your own gear into the store, or you can ask to borrow gear from the retailer for this purpose—most reputable outfitters are happy to lend you gear in order to help ensure that you will purchase the pack most suitable to your needs.

Once you try on a pack, loosen the suspension straps and loosely buckle the chest and hip belts. Bend over, hoist the pack so the hip belt lies directly over the crest of your hipbones, then tighten the belt so that it fits snugly and won't slide down. Next, assume a posture similar to one you would take when hiking. Then tighten the compression straps (alongside the pack) and the load-lifters, which lie at the crest of the shoulder and are responsible for shifting the weight off the top of your shoulders toward the front. Tighten the shoulder straps and, if desired, the chest strap. With all the initial adjustments made, you should feel about two-thirds of the pack's weight on your hips, with the rest evenly distributed between your back and shoulders.

Take a hike around the store and pay attention to how well the pack is shaped to the contours of your back and whether it stays in place when you move side to side and up and down. When correctly fitted, a well-suited pack should add to your overall stability, which is especially important when traveling on skis or snowshoes or when covering slippery terrain.

On the trail, adjust your suspension system to stay comfortable as the terrain changes. When going uphill, you'll want increased mobility in your hips and legs. Achieve that by slightly loosening the hip belt and load-lifters. When going downhill, you'll want everything well stabilized to help you maintain balance. Increase stabilization by tightening everything so that your pack is a mere extension of your body.

Loading Your Pack

The way a pack is loaded affects comfort as much as the fit does. You'll want to be sure it is correctly loaded and also be organized about your packing so you know where things are when you need them (see figure 5.1). The sign of a

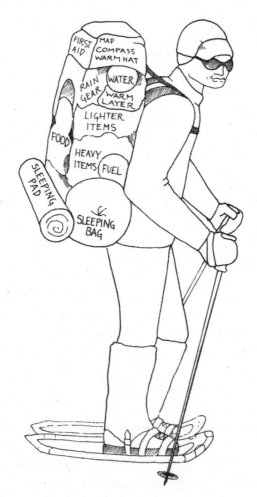

Fig. 5.1. By loading your pack as shown, you will feel more comfortable on your journey.

well-packed sack is its ability to sit up straight when fully packed. Remember the following as you pack:

- Loosen all compression straps before putting anything in your pack.
- Pack your sleeping bag at the very bottom of your backpack, packed in a compression stuff sack. (Compression stuff sacks are made with ultralight nylon and have webbing straps that cinch bags evenly, compressing them to nearly half of the initial stuffed size.) If you're heading to a wet location, line the stuff sack with a garbage bag first. If you're taking a day hike and not carrying a sleeping bag, pack extra clothing at the bottom of your pack.
- Pack heavy items and food directly above your sleeping bag so that the weight rests in the center of your back.
- Put the rest of your items, such as your rain gear, above the food.
- Keep your warm, insulating layer near the top of the pack so you can put it on as soon as you take a break.
- Carry things in a pocket that you want to access quickly, such as a map and compass, first-aid kit, snack food, and an extra hat.
- Make sure the fuel is below any food you might be carrying. That way, the fuel will not leak on the food if it accidentally leaks at all.
- Fill dead air space with small items you won't need to access on short notice, such as a toiletry kit or book.
- Keep all your small items together in a stuff sack if your pack has few pockets—or none at all—in order to stay organized.
- Tighten down all compression straps before setting out.

Child Carriers

Child carriers can be just as comfortable as backpacks if they fit correctly. Look for one that has ample padding for both you and your baby. It should have restraining straps that go over your child's shoulder and around your child's waist, and it should be easily adjustable: your child will grow after all! Make sure it has at least one pouch for carrying water, snacks, and other small items. And check the carrier's load limit to make sure it fits your needs.

Sleds

If you plan on heading into gentle, rolling terrain or traversing long expanses of snowy flats, you may want to exchange your big backpack for a sled. Small sleds used for hauling gear are often called pulks and are particularly advantageous over backpacks when your load is hefty and the snow is super deep. Sleds are also favored by those with back or shoulder pain and by parents wanting to haul their little tykes along on winter adventures. Of course, not all people have the luxury of choosing between a heavy pack or a pulk—on extended trips, you'll likely need both.

Whether you make your own pulk or purchase one manufactured particularly for hauling gear, you should load it with care. Line the pulk with a tarp (especially when traveling in wet climates) and place heavier items low and slightly to the rear. You may prefer to pack your items in a duffel bag and then place it directly on the sled. You can also wrap your load with a space blanket to keep snow and moisture out. Lastly, secure everything by wrapping a bungee cord around the load.

Sleds are particularly useful for pulling small children who aren't yet ready for a long hike, such as this bundled child in the White Mountains, New Hampshire.

To make your own gear-hauling pulk, retrofit a molded plastic sled that you can find at a local toy or sporting goods store. Be sure you buy a sled that is relatively flat. Drill 10 to 12 holes spaced at 1-foot intervals along the top of the sled side-wall, then thread a length of rope through the holes, starting at the top, rounding around the end, and coming back up the other side. Next, take the two ends of the rope and snake them through two PVC pipes, which should be about 5 feet long and have a ¾-inch diameter.

Step 1. Drill 10 to 12 holes and thread rope through them.

Step 2. Run the rope through PVC pipes.

Step 3. Tie loops at the ends of the rope.

PVC pipes should have a ¾-inch diameter and be 5 feet long

Step 4. Clip carabiners to the loops.

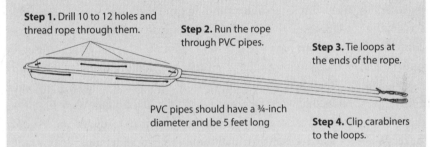

The rigidity of the pipe will prevent the pulk from slamming against your heels as you descend, but make sure both pipes are the same length so that the pulk travels in a straight line and doesn't pull to one side. Tie loops in each rope end, clip a carabiner to each loop, and latch the carabiners to the waist belt of your backpack. For better tracking and control, cross the pipes between the sled and your pack and reinforce the intersection with rope or another carabiner.

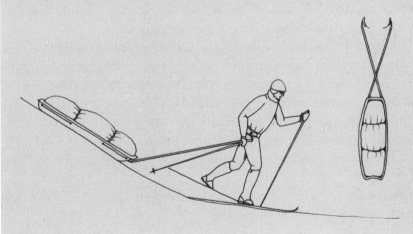

Hydration Systems

There is a cold, hard fact about winter hiking and camping that irks even the most experienced: you can't drink snow. Not only that, but you must actively work to keep your drinking water from freezing when temperatures drop below 32 degrees. You can't keep your bottle in the side pocket of your pack and expect its water to remain liquefied, so you need to either keep it insulated inside your pack or inside an insulated water bottle sleeve attached to the side of your pack.

Until recently, we refused to bring hydration systems such as CamelBaks into the backcountry in winter, as frozen water tends to clog hoses and freeze bite valves shut. These hydration systems consist of an outer shell, an inner water reservoir, and a drinking tube extending from the water reservoir to aid in the sipping of water through the mouthpiece bite valve. These systems are super convenient, as you won't have to dig through your pack to find your bottle every time you want water. Without them, it's more difficult to drink as frequently as you should. When hydration companies recently started making insulated bladders and hoses that won't freeze, we made the investment. We're happy we did. However, we still carry a backup water supply in an insulated water-bottle jacket. When we lead teens, who usually don't have enough money to buy fancy hydration systems, we all follow the simpler methods of keeping our water in bottles. Whichever way you choose, keep in mind some basic guidelines.

A hydration system won't freeze when the drink tube and bite valve are insulated. Older and less-expensive models don't come with insulation, which means you have to provide it yourself. It is possible to jury-rig together an insulated hydration system by wrapping your drinking hose with pipe insulation. An alternative method is to uncoil the drinking tube and have it run along your arm within your clothing so that your body heat prevents freezing. However, this becomes a hassle when adding and removing layers.

Whether you've improvised your own insulation system or bought the newest, beefiest one on the market, it could still freeze on the coldest days if you don't take the following precautions. When the temperature dips really low, fill the bladder with hot water that you've heated over the stove or fire. After taking a few sips, blow air into the tube to force the water out so that it won't freeze. Keep the system close to your body. Always, always have a backup water bottle filled with warm water that you carry upside down in an insulated water bottle jacket. Because some cold air will inevitably enter through the zipper at the top of the insulated water bottle jacket, placing the bottle upside down will ensure that the bottle's lid will not freeze shut.

Water Bottles

It's perfectly acceptable to forego the hydration system altogether and use only water bottles. We each keep one full water bottle tucked in our pack, close to our body, and another bottle sheltered in an insulated sleeve that we clip to the outside of our pack for easy access. We have led groups of teens who do not own insulated water bottle sleeves. In those cases, we have everyone wear their bottles around their necks, tucked against their bodies under their clothing. To do this, cut pieces of cordon approximately 36 inches long, tie the pieces' ends to the lids of the water bottles and make necklaces out of the cordon so that the water bottle hangs down below the sternum like a large pendant. We often have to remind students repeatedly to tuck the bottle back under their clothes after drinking, but it usually becomes second nature after a few rest breaks. When they've slurped down the last of the water around their necks, they transfer water from the bottle in their pack to the bottle around their neck and—voila!—they have another 16 ounces of liquid hydration.

Ice Axes and Crampons

If you plan to limit your winter outings to flat, snowy expanses or gently rolling terrain, you may never need to know about ice axes or crampons, their function, or how they are used. However, more often than not, you'll eventually want to explore steeper slopes and expanded terrain where these tools become standard—and necessary—safety gear. Anyplace where the danger of falling and sliding far enough to hurt yourself exists, you'll need an ice ax and crampons. Please note that these tools are sharp and potentially dangerous. Seek out the proper training prior to using these tools in the field and be sure you learn and practice correct self-arrest technique. The following information is presented here merely to introduce you to the tools and their functions. It's your responsibility to get the necessary instruction for ice ax and crampon use (see Resources).

Ice axes are tools used for ice climbing and to stop uncontrolled glissades (slides). An ice ax consists of a lightweight, durable metal shaft, a pointed spike at the bottom end, and a head with a pick and adze. Because ice axes vary in length, use the following technique to find the right fit for you: hold the ax loosely with cupped fingers and place your arm straight down against your body; the spike should come to your ankle.

Practice carrying your ice ax on gentle slopes before hitting steep ones where you'll need it. Carry the ax on the uphill side of the trail with the adze pointed

Carefully carry an ice ax with your hand wrapped over the top of the ax and the adze end pointed forward.

forward and the pick pointed back. Loop the hand leash around your wrist—it will prevent you from dropping your ax should your hand lose grip of it—and wrap your palm over the pick near the shaft's balance point, placing your thumb under the adze. Now practice walking with the ax, firmly setting the spike into the snow between each step. You'll notice while walking that the ax functions similar to a trekking pole, aiding your balance and traction. However, its most important function is as a self-rescue tool to prevent uncontrolled slides.

Many outdoor groups teach self-arrest techniques at one-day "snow school" classes and have students practice them again and again until they become in-stinctual. These classes teach students how to walk with an ice ax, instructing them how to switch between hands as they zig-zag up a slope so that the ax is always in the uphill hand. Students practice how to slide sitting or lying down on their backs and the way to stop a slide by flipping onto their bellies while holding their axes across their chests and driving their picks into the snow as a brake. This self-arrest maneuver is acrobatic and somewhat counterintuitive, so it does require significant practice. Snow school classes offer fun, hands-on learning experiences that will give you the skills and confidence you need to master the self-arrest.

Crampon technique for walking on snow is relatively simple. Crampons are made from metal spikes and are worn on boots (or skis) to provide traction on snow and ice. Traditional crampons used on mountaineering boots have twelve points—ten underfoot and two forward-facing at the front—though a variety of crampons are on the market and some have four or six points only. Crampons are either rigid (for rigid boots) or hinged under foot for a wider variety of footwear. Manufacturers also produce crampons for different styles of telemark and alpine touring skis so that skiers can traverse icy slopes with ultimate traction. Crampons can be purchased or rented and should always be fitted to the boot or ski prior to heading into the backcountry.

The general technique for walking with crampons is to maintain a normal gait while keeping your feet flat so that as many crampon spikes as possible grip the snow simultaneously. The steeper the terrain, the more difficult it becomes to use crampons effectively.

The Ten Essentials

As a warm-weather hiker, you've likely heard of the ten essentials—the ten items that are essential to your survival, should an accident occur. The ten essentials were first published in a 1930s newsletter of a Seattle-based outdoor club, and they're meant to apply to backcountry survival any time of year. Always carry the following items on your backcountry excursions:

- *Matches* (or *disposable lighters*) and *fire starters* are handy for starting a fire, which can be used to signal for help, keep you warm, and boost morale. Purchase strike-anywhere matches, carry some sort of striker, such as an emery board, and store them in a waterproof case. Because finding dry kindling in the winter is difficult, carrying a small plastic bag full of fire starters (such as chemical heat tabs or resin-soaked chipped-wood blocks) is imperative.
- *Maps and compasses* will be covered in greater depth in Chapter 6. Many backcountry accidents could be avoided if more people carried maps and knew how to read them in conjunction with a compass. Learning how to use a compass can help you navigate your way through featureless winter landscapes, whiteouts, and thickly forested areas.
- *Light sources*, such as headlamps, are particularly useful during short winter days. You'll want to carry extra batteries and bulbs in a waterproof container.
- *Extra food* is crucial to backcountry survival. Bring foods that are dense and fatty, such as nuts, chocolate, jerky, and energy bars.

- *Extra clothing* is critical in the cold weather months. Bring one or two more insulating layers than you think you'll need.

- *Sun protection*, including the aforementioned sunglasses, are often forgotten in the winter months when the sun's rays aren't so obvious. Carry sunglasses and sunscreen—you won't regret it.

- *First-aid kits* are essential during an emergency. Every person should carry a personal first-aid kit to tend to personal injuries, such as small cuts and blisters. Group leaders should carry more substantial kits, with everything from sterile gauze pads to ibuprofen. See Appendix C for more information about items to include in first-aid kits.

- *Repair kits and tools* come in handy more often than you'll anticipate. The contents of your tool kit will depend, in part, on what you plan to do. You may want to include safety pins, spare pack clips, stove parts, extra cordage, and, of course, duct tape. Also bring a multipurpose knife, such a Leatherman or Swiss Army knife.

- *Hydration*, more than even food or shelter, is crucial to your survival. Be sure that each person has at least one bottle and remember that finding running water is quite difficult during the winter. If you aren't planning to boil your water, be sure to carry other treatment devices, such as iodine tablets. (Water filters tend to freeze in the winter and should be avoided.)

- *Emergency shelter* should come along even on day trips when you plan to be channel surfing by nightfall. When you're not carrying a tent, pack a space blanket or tarp and nylon cord.

We would add a *snow shovel* to the list and make eleven essentials if the list were winter-specific. A snow shovel can be used to dig snow caves or snow trenches—essential for surviving a cold, stormy night. Snow shovels, along with *avalanche transceivers* and *avalanche probes*, become requisite items when traveling in avalanche terrain (see Chapter 10).

There is one more personal item you shouldn't leave home without—lip balm. A few years ago we led a group of teens on a snowfield traverse one cloudy day, then descended into a forested area, situated them a half mile apart on an overnight solo expedition, then checked on them halfway through the 12-hour period. When we approached one student and gave her the thumbs-up sign, she wildly beckoned us over to her shelter. "Something's wrong with my lips!" she cried. Sure enough, her lips were fat and blistered. It turns out she hadn't applied any lip balm or sunscreen to her lips the previous day, and she was now suffering the consequences. From that day forward, she always had the most lubed lips of the bunch. The lesson? Remember your lip balm and don't let

Hand and toe warmers are small packets that provide heat on demand. There are many different types of chemical warmers on the market; some last a mere 20 minutes while others produce heat for up to 24 hours, and some are disposable while others are reusable. Hikers and skiers commonly use them to aid in warming the extremities. While they often provide people with increased comfort, we usually ask students not to carry chemical warmers on camping trips; in our experience kids too often rely on them to keep their hands warm, forgetting the basics about staying warm through proper layering, nutrition, and exercise. (Once they've blown through their stash of warmers, these kids usually find the cold much more difficult to bear than other students who had never used hand warmers and instead learned the basics.) Should you choose to bring hand and toe warmers into the backcountry, be sure that you don't become entirely reliant on them to help you stay warm. And, as with anything you bring into the backcountry, remember to pack them out with you at the end of your trip.

cloud cover fool you. Ultraviolet rays reflect off snow with more intensity than they do off any other surface.

Optional Gear

Our friend Megan refuses to go into the backcountry without at least three bandanas, our old co-worker Randy won't go anywhere snowy without stuffing all his gear in dry bags, our buddy Shane can't deny himself his cell phone (even when he knows there won't be reception), and we can't tell you how many kids balk at the idea of setting foot in the snow without first stuffing every pocket with hand warmers. We each have our own little personal items that make us comfortable and happy, and bringing them into the backcountry is generally OK. Just be sure that you can keep your stuff dry, and that it won't weigh you down or give you a false sense of security.

Gear to Leave at Home

There are some items that you should not take into the backcountry. If you doubt whether or not you will be able to carry it for the duration of your trip, leave it at home. The Leave No Trace principles remind us that we're responsible for everything we bring into the woods, including our food packaging. Tin foil, aluminum cans, and plastic bottles, for example, are all things that you should refrain from bringing into the backcountry, as they're cumbersome and difficult to carry out. You will also want to avoid bringing an excessive amount of alcohol. While there's nothing wrong with enjoying a little nip of whiskey in your hot chocolate before bed, you shouldn't carry large bottles or cans of alcohol. Drinking alcohol can contribute to dehydration, and you wouldn't want to be dehydrated *and* responsible for lugging around an empty bottle of alcohol.

CHAPTER SIX

On the Go

Spirits soared on the last morning of our 72-day expedition in Patagonia, Chile, back in 1998. Finally, after all those cold and blustery days without fresh food or new faces, we were only a few miles from showers and vegetables, music and mail. From our first rest break of that last day, we could even make out our destination—it wasn't far at all! We consulted the map, just to be sure we had our bearings, then stuffed our mouths full of all our remaining food, even though it was well before lunch. Carrying extra food just meant carrying extra weight, and we'd had enough. It was time to go home.

The first mile or so went just as planned. Fit and fired up, we all but skipped our way toward our destination. Suddenly a cliff rose before us, stopping us in our tracks. "Where'd that come from?" one person asked. "That's not supposed to be here!" another cried. Sure enough, the cliff was nowhere on the map. But then again, we knew we were traveling in very remote terrain and that our map's contour lines indicated changes in elevation only every 100 meters. The cliff appeared to reach some 99.9 meters into the sky. First we tried climbing up it, but it was too steep. Then we tried going around it to the east, but that didn't work. Finally, frustrated and deflated, we retraced our steps back to our earlier rest spot, chose a new bearing, and then began the long, arduous trek up and around the cliff band.

We finally stumbled upon our destination long after nightfall. We were tired, hungry, cold, wet, and ashamed of ourselves for ending such an empowering expedition on such a poor note. But at least we were alive, which may not have been the case if the temperature was lower or the conditions more extreme. If someone had slipped and fell, all our lives would have been in jeopardy.

While we're not proud to recount this story, it does serve as a reminder of the common mistakes we can all learn from. Hopefully, by presenting you with the following information, we can spare you from making the same mistakes we did. Among other lessons learned from that experience, we always get the most accurate maps available (which is easy to do in the United States and Canada) and we never eat all our food, no matter how close the trailhead appears to be! We've since honed our map and compass skills, learned to anticipate the weather and snow conditions, and become more adept at staying warm and dry. The following information, combined with a healthy dose of experience, will help you on your way.

Staying on Trail

The easiest and best way to stay on track is to keep to the trail. Stay on high-use or easily identifiable trails, especially if you are a beginner, and hone your map and compass skills before you need to use them. Experienced winter hikers can explore more remote trails once they have strong orienteering skills. Trail finding becomes more challenging when the trail is covered in snow, but there are some easy trail identifiers to help you find your way. In high-use areas, snowshoe or ski tracks indicate the route. If you're the first to hit the trail after it has snowed, look for a line of depression—the snow will not be as deep in the trail as it is along the outside of the trail. In wooded areas, a tree-free corridor usually indicates a trail.

If you think you may have lost the trail, stop immediately. Scan your surroundings and try to identify the last point where you know you were on the trail. For example, you might notice a tall, dead tree in the distance or a sharp turn you took. Return there and, if you are able to see where the trail *actually* leads, go ahead and take the trail toward your destination. If you can't see a clear trail continuing from that point, take the trail back to the trailhead. It's better to take a shorter hike than it is to venture on without knowing where you're going.

Realistic Mileage Goals

There is no tried and true method of calculating mileage goals per day, as so many variables exist, such as elevation gain, snow conditions, group fitness, and weather, to name a few. As a very general rule, a fit person can hike about one mile per hour on flat terrain in the winter when carrying a 40-pound pack. It usually takes that same person one hour to gain 1,000 feet in elevation. These estimates merely figure travel time, so you must also account for rest breaks, which you should take at least every half hour. Let's say you hit the trail at

9 A.M. and want to return to your car by 3 P.M. You could choose a route that is approximately 4 miles round trip on flat terrain, or a route that is 2 miles with elevation gain of 2,000 feet. We recommend that you err on the side of shorter hikes if you're just starting out. You'll quickly learn how fast you like to travel, so you can adjust your mileage goals for subsequent hikes.

Maps and Compasses

You may use a map and compass during non-wintertime adventures, but you probably rely on the trail and the easily identifiable landscape features far more. This is understandable—navigating is much easier without snow! When snow covers trails and fills the sky—obstructing landscape views and blanketing lakes, rivers, and drainages—having sharp map and compass skills is imperative. In some winter conditions, they're the only tools that will help you stay found.

A map and compass refresher is a good idea before any hike, and it's especially important when planning a winter outing. Have everyone in your party join the review session, as everyone can help refine each other's skills. If some members of your group haven't learned the fundamentals of map and compass skills, that won't disqualify them from venturing into the backcountry in winter. However, it does mean other members of the group should be map and compass

These young hikers are checking their map and compasses to be sure they're following the correct bearing toward their destination.

experts and be able to share their skills with those who aren't. The map and compass activities included in this chapter will help beginners learn the basics, but they are not a substitute for taking a course in backcountry navigation.

Topographical Maps

Let's start with maps. As described in Chapter 2, topographical (topo) maps put out by the United States Geological Survey (USGS) are best for backcountry travel in the United States. Topo maps are two-dimensional representations of three-dimensional portions of the earth, and the most useful topo maps are those with a 1:24,000-scale, 7.5-minute quadrangle, called quads. Topo maps have contour lines, which are brown lines on the map used to determine elevations. Each contour is a line of equal elevation, so contours never cross. Contour lines stacked together represent steep slopes, while contour lines spaced a little farther apart represent gentler slopes. If the lines are placed far from each other, the terrain is flat.

The contour interval (indicated at the bottom of the map) indicates the distance between each contour line. If, for example, the contour interval is 50 feet, the difference in elevation between every contour line is 50 feet. To help determine elevations, maps show wider, darker index contours every fourth or fifth line. Any difference in the terrain's elevation that is less than the contour interval will not appear on the map (which is why we were surprised by the steep slope that day in Chile; the contour interval was 100 meters and the change in elevation was less).

Contour lines help you do more than determine the elevation. They also help you "read" the terrain so you can identify the mountains, valleys, streams, and lakes in the area, which can help you determine your location. In order to read the terrain, you'll need to understand how various natural features are represented. The following describes how certain types of terrain are depicted by contour lines:

- *Gentle slopes* are represented by widely spaced contour lines.
- *Cliffs* are represented by closely spaced contour lines.
- *Hills and mountains* are represented with curved circles of decreasing size. The innermost circle represents the hilltop or peak, and is thus the highest elevation.
- *Valleys* are represented in a series of V-shaped curves, with the apex of the V's pointing upstream. If the valley is broad, the contour lines outlining it may take the shape of a U, but the concept remains the same: the apex of the U points upstream.

If you're just learning the basics of reading a topo map, use your hands. Make a fist with your left hand (or right hand if you are left-handed). With a pen in your other hand, draw concentric circles around each one of your knuckles. Start with a tiny circle around the "peak" of the knuckle, then work your way down, drawing wider and wider circles until you reach the "valley" between two knuckles. You'll quickly see how your first represents a mountain range and how that range would be represented on a topo map.

- *Ridges* are represented by U- or V-shaped curves on either side of valleys, with the apex of the U or V pointing downhill.
- *Saddles*, or spaces between peaks, are represented by hourglass-shaped contour lines.

Map Colors and Symbols

The USGS does its mapping using summer's polychromatic landscape, when trees aren't covered with snow and lakes aren't frozen solid. But translating what you see on the map to the monochromatic winter landscape around you is easy. Green areas on the map indicate densely forested or vegetated areas, while blue denotes water, white symbolizes areas devoid of vegetation year-round (including permanent snow fields, glaciers, and rock), and black represents unnatural features, such as buildings and mines. Some features are shown by lines, and they usually correspond in color to areas of similar kind. For example, a blue line denotes a river while a black line shows a road. Note that not all maps are up-to-date, especially where logging roads are indicated. Many logging roads become abandoned and overgrown, so they should not be considered a strong reference point during navigation.

The best way to become a skilled map-reader is by practicing and developing your powers of observation. Pay attention to your surroundings—noting every stream, lake, mountain pass, and meadow—and then find the various features on your map. Notice which way the streams run, where the sun sits in the sky, and from which direction the moon rises. Find the North Star, which hangs directly over the North Pole and makes an excellent navigational tool. Once you're adept at map reading, a topo map's contour lines seem to pop up before you in three dimensions and you'll likely delight in matching the natural features around you to the features on the map. It's an empowering feeling in the thick of the backcountry, with no other humans around, when you know *exactly* where you are.

Compasses

While maps help you identify your location, a compass helps you reach your destination. Although you may use your compass only one time for every ten times you consult your map, it's imperative that you always carry a compass and know how to use it. With a compass, if you don't know where you are, you can use your map to identify the features surrounding you. Then use the compass bearings to determine your location.

You can also use the compass to give directions. For example, you could say, "Follow the drainage 0.5 miles upstream to 2,700 feet. Take a bearing of 216 degrees and head uphill along Raindeer Ridge 1.6 miles to 4,100 feet. Take a bearing of 110 degrees and follow ridge to gain summit." A compass will also help you follow a directional bearing to a place you can't see.

Learning how to use a compass is much more difficult on paper (nearly impossible, in fact) than it is when you have a compass in hand. Do yourself a favor and go get a protractor compass before reading any farther.

Got your compass? Great. Now let's review the parts of a compass and how they work together. First off, the compass needle points north. It should be obvious which end of the needle points north—it's distinguished by red or gold paint or by an arrow on its tip. The compass needle floats in a liquid-filled housing that is engraved with an orienting arrow and parallel north-south lines. It is surrounded by a dial, which is calibrated in one- or two-degree increments. The housing and dial rotate on top of a base plate, which is engraved with a direction-of-travel arrow and an index line. Familiarizing yourself with the compass parts will make using a compass in conjunction with a map much easier.

Now use your compass to orient your map. Place the map on a flat surface, such as the ground, and set your compass on the map and align the long side of the compass with the line on the map that indicates magnetic north. When you've done this, you'll see that the map, the compass, and the terrain will all be aligned with each other. Now that you see where you are on the map, you can look around you and identify visible features—from drainages to ridgelines and summits—and use those features to help determine the easiest way of getting from your current location to your destination. You can choose a general route by looking at the map and the features around you, but in order to maintain a consistent direction of travel toward your destination, you'll have to know how to take and follow a bearing.

A bearing is the directional difference between a hiker's current location to the destination—a difference indicated on the compass in degrees (between 1 and 360). To take your bearing, first align the left edge of the compass with your location on the map, then pivot the compass until the top left edge points to your destination on the map (see figure 6.1). Then, rotate the compass dial so that the parallel north-south lines align with map's north and south lines. Look at the direction of travel index line and see what number it points to. If it points to 130, for example, your bearing is 130 degrees. However, there's one last step—you need to adjust for declination.

Simply stated, declination is the difference, in degrees, between what your compass says is north and what north actually is. Confusing? Your compass needle points to the magnetic north pole, which is hundreds of miles away

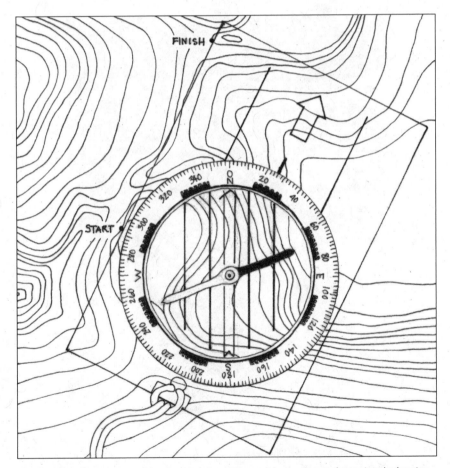

Fig. 6.1. Align the compass with your current position and destination to determine the bearing you will need to take.

from the true North Pole. Your map, on the other hand, indicates true north, so you need to adjust your compass a certain number of degrees depending on your distance from true north. The earth's magnetic field varies depending on location, so every part of the world has a different declination. Declination amounts are listed in the margins of maps.

In the following instructions about adjusting for declination, let's imagine we are in the White Mountains of New Hampshire where the margin of the maps indicates we have a west declination of 16 degrees (meaning the magnetic north on our compasses is 16 degrees west of true north) and have just taken a bearing of 130 degrees. With west declinations, we add the declination amount to our original bearing (as opposed to east declinations, when we would subtract). So, in our case, we add 16 to 130 and get 146 as our final bearing.

Keep your map handy while on the trail and pull it out at regular intervals to stay oriented.

Now that we have a bearing, it's time to follow it and reach our destination. Hold the compass flat in your hand. Turn the dial until the direction of travel index is aligned with 146 degrees. Now rotate the compass until "red is in the shed"—in other words, the compass arrow should be aligned with the orienting arrow. Then look where the direction-of-travel index line is pointing—it's pointing to your destination. Head off in that direction. As you travel, you'll inevitably meander a bit as you negotiate around boulders and stands of trees, so occasionally consult your compass to be sure you're following your bearing. If you reach your destination and decide you want to go somewhere else, just take another bearing and repeat the process. You have the tools to know where you are, where you're going, and how to get there. Though orienteering sounds difficult initially, rest assured that it will become second nature with practice.

Other Tools

If you have—and know how to use—your map and compass, and if you have the ten essentials and a good sense of safety and judgment, you won't need the additional tools we describe here. However, an increasing number of people heading into the backcountry these days rely on the Global Positioning System (GPS) and other technical tools, which is why they warrant a brief discussion. Many of them do help supplement the map and compass, facilitate navigation, or make it easier to anticipate changing weather conditions.

Global Positioning Systems

The Global Positioning System is the world's largest and most functional global navigation satellite system. Consumers today can purchase GPS receivers in a variety of formats, and they've become increasingly affordable and accurate in the past decade. With good reason, they've also become increasingly popular. A GPS receiver can pinpoint your location on the surface of the earth within just a few feet. This is especially useful in the backcountry when you're traveling on unmarked trails and you're trying to decide whether you're on the north side or south side of a lake. Let's say your GPS receiver confirms that you are, in fact, standing on the north side of the lake, and now you want to travel toward a peak located to the southeast. A GPS receiver can tell you which way is north, south, east, and west, but it can't plot out a route that works with the landscape's unique variations; in other words, you still need to plot a route on your map. Once you've done that, you can enter various waypoints into your GPS and it will tell you in which direction to walk.

Never, *ever* rely on these tools in lieu of a map and compass. Just imagine if the batteries in your GPS receiver were to run out, or if someone in your group were to accidentally step on your altimeter. These things do happen, so you'd better be able to forge ahead with old-fashioned, time-honored navigational tools.

Altimeters and Barometers

Many technical outdoor watches today come with an altimeter and a barometer, both of which can be quite useful in the backcountry. Altimeters read barometric pressure to measure vertical distances above sea level, so they determine your elevation and help you locate your position. The best altimeters are accurate within 10 feet, but you'll want to cross-reference their readings with maps and trail signs to be sure they are correct. Our altimeter watches are a little old, and we often find ourselves resetting the altimeter depending on what the map and trail markers tell us.

Changes in barometric pressure help you anticipate changing weather conditions and plan accordingly. Air, as you know, has weight, and a barometer measures changes in air pressure. If air pressure is high or rising (and thus your barometer reading is high or rising), the weather should stay dry for the next 12 to 24 hours, though temperature may be very cold. If the barometer reading is low or falling, expect wet weather: the lower reading, the stronger storm. While you should always be prepared for inclement weather, knowing when a big storm is coming is helpful—you may want to modify your route, and you'll definitely want to take extra care when setting camp for the night.

Winter Weather

Four days into a week-long February camping trip near Sunday River Ski Resort in Maine, the teenage boys we were leading were getting lazy. Since we had hit the trail, the skies had been clear and the temperature mild. The snow was just a few feet deep and well packed, capped with a layer of hardened crust that made snowshoeing no more difficult than walking. Some days, the guys didn't even bother to put on their hats or mittens as we made good time on the trail. They threw snowballs at each other and joked about how easy and fun this all was—how lame we'd been to insist they bring so much extra clothing and gear. In camp each night, their tarps became increasingly saggy and they set anchors as an afterthought, positive that no wind or weather would blow down their shelters. We warned them, but they didn't care to listen. Only experience could teach them.

When the snow is deep and more keeps falling, you sometimes have to put your head down and keep going at a slow, steady pace.

Snow started falling in the middle of the fourth night. It came down fast and thick, quickly piling around our tent and the teens' tarps. While the boys continued to sleep, we quietly checked their shelters, which were sagging and leaning every which way, and determined that they would stand through the night.

When we woke the boys up the next morning, they looked wide-eyed and scared. The snow and cold we'd warned them about had finally arrived, and they feared they wouldn't fare well in the challenging conditions. For the first time, they listened with great attention and hung on our every word. *What are we supposed to do? How are we supposed to get warm?* The morning routine took twice as long as normal, and it was slow going when we finally did hit the trail. The snow kept falling and the wind picked up. Then the snow stopped. The temperature rose. The sleet started. As we kept traveling, the conditions kept changing. "This is hard," one young man complained during a rest break. It was true. Traveling is more difficult when the conditions aren't dry and sunny. But changing conditions are what winter is all about. We reminded the students how awesome they were to be able to safely travel and camp in such conditions, relying solely on their bodies, their skills, and the equipment they could carry on their backs. Within a few hours, they started believing they were "hard core" and could conquer anything if they paid attention and worked together. They learned that winter weather is dynamic and nature puts on some of her most impressive spectacles during the coldest time of year. They learned that in order to appreciate the beauty, anticipate changing conditions, and understand how those conditions affect a hiker's ability to travel efficiently, knowing the basics about winter weather is essential.

In short, winter weather can range from mild and sunny to stormy and bitterly cold, with precipitation including everything from freezing rain and sleet to snow and ice. While conditions may seemingly change out of the blue with no forewarning, that's not usually the case. It's a good idea to learn about the regional climate and weather patterns of the place you're visiting before even setting foot there. In the Northeast, for example, clear skies and cold temperatures characterizes winter weather, which is punctuated with occasional storms that drop masses of dry snow. The coldest month of the year in New England is typically mid-January to mid-February, a time during which high-pressure systems move in from the northwest, bringing clear skies and temperatures below zero. While the forecast may change day to day, and seasonal variations may be strong, weather patterns in a given area generally remain consistent year to year. You may learn that winds constantly whip through a certain mountain pass, or that they generally come from a particular direction. Information like this can help you determine your route and make decisions about things such as the direction your tent will face.

Once you're in the backcountry, a keen sense of observation can help you read all the messages that clouds—along with wind, changing temperatures,

The dark clouds approaching this New Hampshire winter scene foreshadow precipitation and changing weather conditions.

and air pressure—send throughout the day. By picking up on those messages, you can be prepared for changing weather conditions. Plus, those who tinker in amateur meteorology generally find their backcountry experience more rewarding. The sky alone can be just as entertaining as your favorite TV show. Clouds reveal the sky's secrets. A basic cloud refresher will help you understand how.

- *Cirrus clouds* are characterized by thin, wisplike strands (also known as "mares' tails") composed of ice crystals that form at high elevations of about 18,000 feet. They generally occur during fair weather and point in the direction of air movement at their elevation.

Cirrus clouds

Stratus clouds

Cumulus clouds

Lenticular clouds

Cumulonimbus clouds

Halo

- *Cumulus clouds* are your fair-weather friends. Puffy and white, they are usually as benign as the ones you drew in kindergarten with white crayons. The worst weather they forecast is light wind.
- *Cumulonimbus clouds* are similar to cumulus clouds but are thicker, darker, and more tower-like than their benign brothers. These clouds tell of a coming storm.
- *Stratus clouds* appear like sheets on the horizon, moving low and fast in horizontal layers. Often accompanied by strong wind, they usually signal a change in the weather—a storm coming or going.
- *Lenticular clouds* are the wispy white caps that hover over peaks. They indicate that high-elevation terrain is getting slammed with high, cold wind, and their presence generally forewarns precipitation within 48 hours.

Ice crystal halos are another atmospheric optical phenomenon that can indicate changing weather. They usually form in high cirrus clouds, often circling the sun or moon, and tell of coming precipitation. Wide halos indicate that precipitation is a day or two away, while tight halos signify that precipitation is imminent.

If you know about weather, you probably know that fronts are masses of air and that warm and cold fronts (warm and cold masses of air) interact in various ways to affect weather. When a warm front moves into an area, warm air amasses over the cold air already in place and clouds form. Those clouds may thicken and drop precipitation if the warm air rises quickly. In the Northeast, for example, big winter storms called nor'easters occur when warm fronts from the southwest enter over and converge with cold fronts from the Arctic air mass in the northwest. Nor'easters usually result in massive amounts of precipitation and high winds. If you plan to set out into the northeastern backcountry when the forecast calls for a low-pressure front to enter in from the southwest, you should be prepared for dynamic storms and fast, drastic weather changes or postpone your trip until the nor'easter has passed.

We've all experienced how much colder the temperature feels when wind is whipping around us. Unlike summertime, when we welcome wind for its ability to cool us off and rid an area of mosquitoes, wintertime causes us to loathe the wind. Aside from shaping beautiful snow sculptures, the only thing wind does that we notice is suck away our heat, chap our cheeks, blow snow in our eyes, and zap our energy reserves. A perfectly comfortable 15-degree afternoon can feel like an excruciatingly cold minus-7 degrees when the wind blows at 35 miles per hour.

The Wind Chill Index

By utilizing the wind chill index, which was most recently revised in 2000, you can figure out how the wind speed affects the temperature and thus how fast frostbite can occur on exposed skin at that wind chill temperature.

Temperature (°F)

Wind (mph)	40	35	30	25	20	15	10	5	0	-5	-10	-15	-20	-25	-30	-35	-40	-45
5	36	31	25	19	13	7	1	-5	-11	-16	-22	-28	-34	-40	-46	-52	-57	-63
10	34	27	21	15	9	3	-4	-10	-16	-22	-28	-35	-41	-47	-53	-59	-66	-72
15	32	25	19	13	6	0	-7	-13	-19	-26	-32	-39	-45	-51	-58	-64	-71	-77
20	30	24	17	11	4	-2	-9	-15	-22	-29	-35	-42	-48	-55	-61	-68	-74	-81
25	29	23	16	9	3	-4	-11	-17	-24	-31	-37	-44	-51	-58	-64	-71	-78	-84
30	28	22	15	8	1	-5	-12	-19	-26	-33	-39	-46	-53	-60	-67	-73	-80	-87
35	28	21	14	7	0	-7	-14	-21	-27	-34	-41	-48	-55	-62	-69	-76	-82	-89
40	27	20	13	6	-1	-8	-15	-22	-29	-36	-43	-50	-57	-64	-71	-78	-84	-91
45	26	19	12	5	-2	-9	-16	-23	-30	-37	-44	-51	-58	-65	-72	-79	-86	-93
50	26	19	12	4	-3	-10	-17	-24	-31	-38	-45	-52	-60	-67	-74	-81	-88	-95
55	25	18	11	4	-3	-11	-18	-25	-32	-39	-46	-54	-61	-68	-75	-82	-89	-97
60	25	17	10	3	-4	-11	-19	-26	-33	-40	-48	-55	-62	-69	-76	-84	-91	-98

Frostbite Times ■ 30 minutes ■ 10 minutes ■ 5 minutes

Wind Chill (°F) = 35.74 + 0.6215T − 35.75(V^{0.16}) + 0.4275T(V^{0.16})

$$\text{Wind Chill (°F)} = 35.74 + 0.6215T - 35.75(V^{0.16}) + 0.4275T(V^{0.16})$$

Where T = Air Temperature (°F), V = Wind Speed (mph)

Snow Conditions

Say the word "snow" and immediately a white image jumps to mind, though the image may be very different depending on where you live and what snow conditions you're used to. Snow falls in many different variations, depending on its moisture content. As a general rule, moisture content is higher in maritime climates and regions where the air temperature is warmer; moisture content is generally lower in inland mountainous regions or very cold regions such as the northeastern United States. And the quality of the snow may change once it hits the ground and piles up, depending on the weather conditions it is exposed to. The various conditions of snowpack—powder, crust, corn, slush, and ice—will affect the way you travel.

Powder is ideal for downhill skiers. It's freshly fallen, soft, and pristine, and it's common in cold regions such as the Northeast, and in inland mountain ranges such as the Rockies. While skiers and snowboarders find it *the* ultimate surface for fast descents, snowshoers and cross-country skiers note that powder can be challenging to plow through when it's deep and unconsolidated. After a heavy snowfall of light powder, it won't consolidate enough for easy travel for several days. Even beginning and intermediate downhill skiers get frustrated with powder because you have to move quickly in order to avoid getting stuck. The wider your skies or snowshoes, the better you'll float on top of powder and not sink. If the powder is deep and you keep postholing (breaking through the surface), consider traveling at night or early in the morning when the snow has a frozen surface. Or look for shady areas that the sun's rays have yet to reach. If snow reports call for a significant amount of powder, reduce your mileage goals—the scenery will be gorgeous but the going will be slow.

Crust is just what the name implies—a type of snow with a harder crust above a softer powder. Crust is formed when the top layer of powder refreezes after it has been melted by sun and wind. If the crust is thin and relatively soft, you'll easily punch through it on snowshoes (and possibly even on skis), but if it's hard you'll ride on top of it. Traveling over crust is most frustrating when it alternates from being soft to being hard, as you'll be contentedly riding on top of it one moment, then punching through the next.

Corn snow is wet and granular and typically found during spring conditions or in maritime climates. Corn snow is the result of the cycle of nightly freezing and daily thawing that happens in the spring. When the temperature is low and corn snow holds its form, it makes for good ski and snowshoe conditions. However, if the temperature continues to rise, the snow melts more and more and becomes sloppy and heavy like mashed potatoes.

Wet, slushy snow likes to stick to everything—including the clothes on this small child, who is happily bundled up in a sled for a winter journey.

Slush is melting snow—the mucky stuff that comes after corn. It's heavy, quite wet, and very difficult to maneuver through, whether you're on skis or snowshoes.

Ice is the most dreaded form of frozen water on trails and slopes, loathed by experienced skiers and snowboarders with the same fervency as they love powder. Ice is hard and slippery and causes treacherous—and potentially dangerous—travel. When anticipating icy conditions, make sure your snowshoe cleats are in good condition. If you plan to ski, carry ski crampons and know how to put them on your skis and use them on the slopes. If the ice is particularly slippery or you feel your safety is at all jeopardized by the conditions, it's time to retreat.

Traveling Over Frozen Water

One of the great pleasures of winter travel in the northern United States is the opportunity to traverse directly across the wide, frozen lakes that you would otherwise have to hike around in warmer seasons. Covered with wind-packed

If you should fall into icy water, try to stay calm and act quickly. Swim to an edge of ice that you think looks thick enough to sustain your weight. Extend your forearms over the ice and try to get your body nearly horizontal by aggressively kicking the water with powerful frog-like strokes. Continue kicking with your legs and pull your lower body to the surface until you are out of the water. Do not attempt to pull with your arms only, as they will slip. Once out, get changed into dry clothing as soon as possible and seek treatment for shock and hypothermia.

snow, the slick, flat, hard surface makes for fast terrain, the wide-open vistas provide jaw-dropping scenery, and you're more likely to catch sight of wildlife when you're near waterways. But be aware that ice travel can be just as hazardous as it is enticing.

Evaluate the ice conditions before even setting a foot (or ski) onto a frozen surface. Step back and think about the recent weather conditions. If there has recently been a significant warming period or a thaw, or if you're approaching a lake during early winter or spring, the ice is probably not stable. Even in the deep cold of midwinter, exercise caution before putting any body weight on the ice. Test it by giving it a firm blow with one end of your trekking pole. If the resulting sound is a substantial thump, it suggests solid ice of at least one inch thick (the minimum thickness that supports the average person's weight). If it doesn't sound solid, step away and find an alternate route around the lake. Also step away if you notice tributary streams nearby—their current will keep ice from freezing solid in even the coldest temperatures.

Only cross a lake when you are sure that it is frozen solid. If all signs are favorable and you decide to venture onto the ice, do so with caution. As you do when crossing a river in summer or traversing a potential avalanche slope in winter (see Chapter 10), unbuckle your pack's hip belt and sternum strap so that you can shed it if necessary. Use your ski poles to tap the ice ahead as you go. If the tapping from your poles reverberates with a hollow sounding "bonk," retreat to land. If it reverberates with a solid "thump," continue moving, avoiding areas with objects, such as logs, jutting from the ice (these areas are often weak). If a large portion of a lake is under the shadow of cliffs or trees, stay in that area—the sun doesn't penetrate shadow lands as often, so ice there tends to be thicker. When in a group, spread out to disperse weight.

Staying Warm and Dry

When you're on the go, it's easy to get caught up in the moment. There are so many sights to see—from birch branches dripping with icicles to snow-swept mountain vistas. There's the rush of adrenaline as you travel, your body generating warmth even as the crisp cold nips at your nose. You barely notice that you're starting to perspire beneath your layers, that you haven't had a sip of water in over an hour, and that you last ate before even hitting the trailhead.

You are your most effective tool in the backcountry. If you can keep yourself warm, dry, and hydrated, you'll thrive—and your brain will be functioning well enough that you will be able to navigate well and reap the benefits of winter adventuring. It does take a concentrated effort to stay warm and dry when you're on the go. While taking a break from writing this book, we headed out on an easy day hike into the Cascade Mountains and kept notes along the way so we could share our experience with you. The following is an account of our day-trip adventure:

5:30 A.M.   Alarm rings. Time to get up. Drink some water.

6:00 A.M.   Oatmeal breakfast. This is good stick-to-the-ribs grub to get us energized.

6:30 A.M.   Final check through each other's equipment to be sure we each have our ten essentials and the additional gear we'll need for the day.

6:45 A.M.   Drive toward the trailhead. On our way, we call a relative and let her know where we plan to go, what equipment we have with us, and when we plan to be back.

7:45 A.M.   Arrive at the Kelcema Lake trailhead. Stretch. Drink some water. Pee. Strap on snowshoes. Check the map.

8:00 A.M.   Hit the trail.

8:10 A.M.   Stop briefly to take off a layer. Drink some water. Check the map.

8:45 A.M.   Rest break. Put on an insulating layer. Eat some trail mix. Drink some water. Go pee. Check the map.

8:55 A.M.   Remove insulting layer and head back to the trail.

9:45 A.M.   Starts snowing lightly. Pause to put on waterproof shell. Drink some water.

10:30 A.M.   Rest break. Put on insulating layer. Eat an energy bar. Drink some water. Consult the map. Go pee. Yemaya checks a hot spot on her right foot and adjusts the sock that's bunched up around her heel.

10:45 A.M.   Remove insulting layer and head back to the trail.

11:05 A.M.   Snow stops. Pause to take off waterproof shell.

When the weather is mild, a tired hiker may take a quick nap on the trail.

11:45 A.M. Sun coming out. Pause to put on sunscreen and take off hats and mittens. Drink some water. Eat a piece of jerky.

12:30 P.M. Reach Kelcema Lake! Put on an insulating layer. Break for lunch—PB&J sandwiches, carrots, yogurt-covered pretzels. Lucas checks to see whether lake solid enough to traverse and decides against it. Consult the map. Go pee.

1:00 P.M. Remove insulating layer and return to the trail, heading back toward trailhead.

1:30 P.M. Pause to drink some water and soak in the views.

2:00 P.M. Rest break. Put on an insulating layer. Eat some more trail mix. Drink some water. Go pee.

2:10 P.M. Remove insulating layer and return to the trail.

2:45 P.M. Clouds cover sun and threaten more snow. Temperature drops. Pause to put on waterproof shell, hat, and mittens. Drink some water.

3:30 P.M. Return to trailhead as snow begins dumping down.

Our Kelcema Lake day-trip journal may sound a little bland, but you get the point—staying warm and dry on even an easy adventure like this one requires constant attention to layering, hydration, nutrition, first aid, and navigation.

Every time we stopped, we immediately put on an additional layer, which we then removed as soon as we took up the trail again. When we took a rest break, we always took care to sit on either our packs or the insulating closed-cell foam pads that we brought along for just this purpose. If we did ever get some snow on us (like Lucas when he lost his footing and slipped near the lake) we immediately brushed it off our clothing.

This sort of constant motion takes a while to become second nature. Don't worry—experience is the best teacher. Just remember to bite off only as much as you can chew. The consequences for getting a little cold and wet aren't as severe a few hundred meters from a trailhead as they are a few days' distance from civilization. Become comfortable with day trips and snowshoes before graduating to day trips and skis, if skiing is even your aspiration. Once you have a bundle of successful day trips beneath your belt, then consider spending a night in the backcountry. Overnight trips involve more preparation and demand a greater level of organization because you must get to camp and set up before the sun goes down. For overnight and extended backcountry trips, create a Time Control Plan (TCP) for each day. A TCP provides an outline for all the day's activities, from what time you plan to wake in the morning to what compass bearings you will follow throughout the day to stay on-route. Attempt extended backcountry trips only when you feel confident in your ability to stay warm, dry, and found.

Example Time Control Plan

Coordinators: 1) Lucas St. Clair
                      2) Yemaya Maurer
Map readers: 1) Megan Hirsh
                      2) Chris Henderson
Breakfast cook: Lorenzo Baker
Dinner cook: Jan Baker
Assistant: Todd Crane

Estimated time of departure: 6:30 A.M.

Mileage for the day: 4.4 miles
Elevation gain for day: 1,600 feet
Obstacles: Route finding above tree line. Lots of climbing. Potential for afternoon precipitation.

Estimated time of arrival: 3:30 P.M.

Present location: 600-foot topo line at the bottom of the drainage running
    southwest from the summit Mount Tom
Destination: The north side of Mount Tom at the small, unnamed pond that
    sits at 1,300 feet. Camping in the notch on the north side of the pond in
    the flat area.

Alternate plan
Assess progress at lunch break. If it looks like we won't make it to camp by
    4 P.M., consider camping on South side of Mount Tom near Lower Lake at
    900 feet.

CHAPTER SEVEN

Camping Gear

For the fourth day in a row, three of us hunkered down in our tent for a game of cards as the storm outside raged on. We'd already finished the books we'd brought, had heard each other's philosophical ramblings, and were caught up on each other's lives. Fortunately, we had a deck of cards, a great tent, warm sleeping bags, insulating pads, and plenty of food, water, and warm clothes. Even if the storm surged for another week, we'd survive.

We had left our tent during the previous 72 hours only to shovel snow from its sides, get food and water, and go to the bathroom. Sometimes we opted to urinate in the shell of our plastic mountaineering boots, then poke our heads out the tent's vestibule and pour our pee on the snow. Gross? Yep. But when it's that cold out there, you've got to do what you've got to do. We had to stay warm, dry, and calm. Because we had great gear (including a cheery yellow winter tent), that was relatively easy to do.

You won't usually be holed up in your tent for the majority of your camping trip. Most winter campers want to spend as much time as possible out of camp, although you may also like long, cozy evenings roasting s'mores and sharing stories around a campfire or quiet nights studying the constellations and listening to the hush of falling snow. You can plan your winter camping adventure to be anything you'd like, but in order to execute the plan, you'll need good shelter, strong cooking ware, warm sleeping bags, and extra clothes.

Tents and Tarps

Winter backpacking tents come in a variety of shapes and sizes and all differ from three-season tents because they're heavier (they have more fabric and less

With a good tent and sleeping bag, you can weather even the biggest storms.

mesh in order to withstand winter storms and snow loads), they're larger (to store more gear), and they utilize more poles (to increase their strength).

Most backpacking tent bodies consist of two layers: a waterproof fly stretched over a breathable inner canopy. In theory, the water vapor inside the tent will pass through the canopy, condense on the outer fly, and become water droplets that run down the fly to the ground. A tent will be able to put this theory into practice if it ventilates properly by having a well-made fly with zippered, retractable vents and a fly door that can be opened at the top without letting precipitation in. This is one of many aspects you should consider when choosing the winter tent that is right for you. On the following pages are some questions to ask when evaluating a tent.

How strong is this tent? Winter tents must effectively withstand heavy wind and snow. Four-season (or winter) tents are manufactured to be stronger than their warm-weather counterparts.

How well does this tent shed snow? The roofline of the tent must allow snow to slide off. If snow piles up on your tent, the snow will eventually cause your tent to collapse. (Note that in heavy snowstorms, snow will pile up against your tent's walls, so you still need to go outside and dig occasionally.)

Look inside this taut dome tent, pitched in the Maine Woods, and you'll see the recommended sleeping pad arrangement—a short pad lying on top of a full-length pad.

How much room is there? Winter tents should be large enough to accommodate you, your traveling partners, and all the bulky gear you want to keep dry. Because you could occasionally be snowed in for a few days, you'll want enough room to avoid going stir crazy. Consider both floor space and head space when evaluating room, as some tents have adequate floor space but don't allow more than one person to sit up simultaneously. Also consider the ease of entry and exit and whether there will be enough room for changing clothes and maneuvering into your sleeping bag. We generally recommend choosing a tent with a capacity that is one person greater than the actual number of people in your group. For example, choose a three-person tent if two people will be traveling together—you will have room for your clothing and gear, and the tent will be roomy enough for an additional person if you decide to invite a friend.

How durable is the tent? Evaluate all materials, including fabric, zippers, loops, seams, lash tabs, stakes, and lines to ensure they are strong. Seams should be factory-sealed.

How much does this tent weigh? Additional strength, room, and durability generally adds weight, so you need to find the comfort-weight balance that works for you.

How easy and fast is it to set up and break down this tent? Particularly when the conditions are less than optimal, you'll want to be able to pitch a tent quickly so that its interior won't get wet as you're setting it up or breaking it down.

How easy is it to enter and exit this tent? We find that our feelings about a tent depend in large part on our feelings about its doors. Two doors on opposite ends of the tent are better than only one door for two reasons: if the wind direction changes in the middle of the night, you can still open a door without inviting in a gust of snow; with two doors, occupants can enter and exit the tent without crawling over their tent mates; and two doors offer greater opportunities for ventilation. Some tents have tunnel entrances, which prevent precipitation from entering, but also make it difficult for occupants to exit with grace. To avoid problems if snow builds up against the tent walls, do not purchase tents with zippered entrances. Also avoid doors that fold down when opened, as they tend to drop snow directly into the tent. We prefer tent doors that flip out sideways, tossing snow buildup away from the interior.

Does the fly have a vestibule? A vestibule—like an entry hall—is a covered entrance great for storing gear. We prefer a tent with at least one vestibule where we can remove our boots and gaiters and shake them free of snow before bringing them inside the tent. Some vestibules are built with ventilation domes that are designed for opening when cooking inside the vestibule. This is a dangerous practice and we do not recommend it.

Does the fly door have an "eyelid"? The tops of some fly doors can be left open to allow for ventilation without letting precipitation inside the tent. This feature is called an "eyelid" and it is recommended that your fly door have one (see figure 7.1). In lieu of an eyelid, some tents have vents high up on the fly to serve the same purpose, though they usually let a little precipitation inside.

Does the tent have a "bathtub floor"? In other words, do the sidewall seams rise above the ground? A bathtub floor is preferable to one in which the seams are at the ground level. These seams are problematic be-

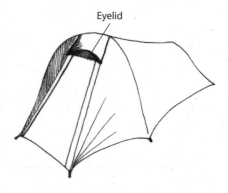

Fig. 7.1. Eyelids allow for ventilation but prevent precipitation from entering the tent.

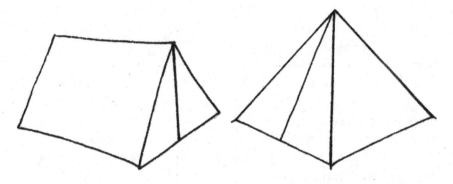

Figs. 7.2 and 7.3. A-frame tents (left) and pyramid tents are still available but have become less common.

cause they receive more stress and become chronic leak points, allowing cold air and precipitation to get in.

How packable is this tent? Consider the amount of room the tent will take up in your backpack and how easy splitting the load between two people seems.

How useful—and usable—are the features? Examine all the pockets, zippers, poles, and location and type of tie-outs.

You'll also need to make a decision about tent body design. Most winter tents fall into one of the following four categories: hoops, domes, pyramids, or hubs. You'll still see old-fashioned A-frame (see figure 7.2) and single-pole pyramid tents on the market (see figure 7.3). While these are OK for early and late winter hiking when the forecast calls for calm skies, they are inadequate for serious winter camping because they provide little head room and don't function well in strong winds.

Hoop Tents

Hoops—also known as Conestoga wagons—resemble A-frame tents but their poles are inverted U's (not inverted V's). Tents with a hoop design function better than A-frames, but they still have a relatively small amount of fabric supported by poles when compared to dome and hub tents.

Fig. 7.4. Because hoop tents require few poles, they are very light.

Dome Tents

Dome tents, shaped like half-spheres, looks just like their name implies (see figure 7.5). Their interlocking poles provide unparalleled support and strength. The additional poles do add to the tent's weight, but we think the added weight is worth it: a dome tent has about 35 percent more volume than an A-frame tent of the same floor

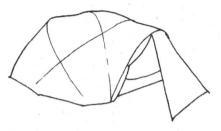

Fig. 7.5. Dome tents weigh more than hoop tents but are stronger and more durable.

area and height. The tent walls are nearly vertical near the ground, allowing occupants to sit up anywhere in the tent. While all dome tents are freestanding (meaning they don't need to be staked into the ground to stand upright), they'll blow away as quickly as a balloon if not properly secured. The benefit of a freestanding tent is that you can easily pick it up and move it without disassembling it—a useful benefit if you realize you've initially pitched on a slope or over a rock.

Hub Tents

Hub tents have a sleeker design than dome tents (see figure 7.6). Their flexible poles branch out from one or more molded plastic hubs, located along the tent's backbone. Because the poles cannot move in relation to each other at their intersection point, these tents are exceptionally rigid and are therefore able to shrug off snow and resist wind effectively. The poles usually attach to the hub (or hubs) at one end with elastic shock cord, which can simplify pitching. Hub tents also have the advantage of being relatively light because some of the poles are shorter than others. A disadvantage of hub tents is that they are not freestanding—they require staking to stand.

Fig. 7.6. Hub tents are exceptionally rigid because the poles lock together where they intersect.

Snow Stakes

Conventional tent stakes do not function in winter conditions. You'll need to purchase snow stakes, which are longer, stouter, and more durable than their fair-weather counterparts. Although some four-season tents include winter stakes, be sure to examine them before making a purchase to be sure they're suitable and have the proper characteristics of snow stakes. Taking a few extra snow stakes with you is advisable. In Chapter 8, you'll also learn other methods of anchoring a tent.

Tarps

Tarps may be preferable to tents if you're looking for a shelter that is lighter, more affordable, and more versatile. If you correctly pitch a tarp, create a sleeping trench beneath it, and seal the area between the ground and the bottom of the tarp with snow, you can create a shelter that is nearly as warm, comfortable, and effective as a tent. When leading groups of young people in the backcountry, we often have them pitch tarps for shelter, and we also carry one four-season tent. (In the event of someone becoming injured or hypothermic, a tent serves as a better shelter—it's quick to pitch and quick to warm).

A tarp shelter can be as simple as a tarp supported by a string of nylon tied to two trees. When trees aren't available, you can also bury one end of a ski in the snow and use the other end like you would use a tree branch. A tarp can also be set up like a teepee, supported by one center pole. Tarps are not freestanding, they don't have walls, and they don't fare well in fierce storms—all disadvantages.

In order to build an adequate tarp shelter, you need to first dig a sleeping trench that is a little longer and wider than you and your gear. Make the walls of your trench splay down at a 45-degree angle so that you have additional room at your structure's base (see figure 7.7). Line the bottom of the trench with a space blanket or ground tarp. String the ceiling tarp at a steep angle over the trench so that it completely covers the sleeping area and shrugs snow away. Secure the tarp with anchors (see Chapter 8) and create a wall of snow on three ends of the tarp to prevent cold air and moisture from entering. Your entrance will be at the open end of the tarp, in front of which you can dig out a "mudroom" for you to put your boots and gaiters before entering your shelter (see Chapter 8).

Huts

If all this talk of tents and tarps makes you feel uneasy, don't let go of your dreams to try winter camping altogether—you could potentially stay in a back-country hut or yurt. Popular chains of huts have blossomed across the country, allowing you the opportunity for a multiday winter excursion without putting forth the effort of setting up camp. Some huts have wood heating stoves, propane cooking stoves, mattresses, and even lights. Just remember, though, you are still responsible for staying warm, dry, and found as you travel between huts. You always need to carry your ten essentials and know how to use them.

Caring for Your Tent

Unless you plan to traverse the polar ice cap, your winter tent will likely spend the majority of its life in storage. Properly stored, your tent will last many, many years. The number one rule to remember is to dry it before you store it to prevent mold and mildew from ruining your perfectly good tent. In some circumstances, you will have to pack up your tent in the field while it's still damp, which is fine as long as you take it out as soon as you return home, set it up, and let it air dry completely. Once it's completely dry, turn the tent inside out and shake it to remove any dirt or food crumbs. When the tent is clean and *completely dry*—we can't reiterate this enough—store it in a cool, dry place away from direct sunlight. Store the poles and stakes in their own bags to reduce the risk of ripping or poking holes in the tent's fabric. Every time you put away your tent, fold it or roll it in a new way so that creases won't develop over time.

Tarps such as these, pitched in the Maine Woods, offer good lightweight, versatile shelters for winter camping.

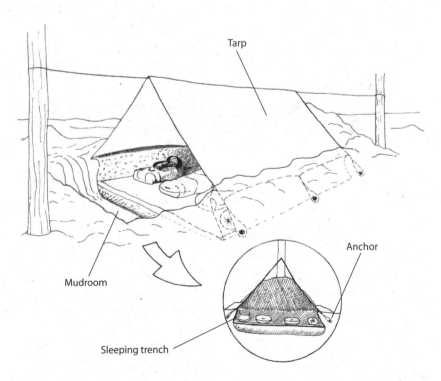

Fig. 7.7. Set up your tarp as shown. Tarp shelters can be nearly as comfortable and warm as tents.

Sleeping Bags

On the few occasions when winter adventuring turns downright miserable—when the weather is cold and wet, when visibility is reduced to mere feet, and when we've already eaten all our favorite foods—our sleeping bags give us hope. We know that after making camp, cooking food, melting snow for water, and closing up camp for the night, we can retreat into our tents and experience the pure bliss of settling into a warm, dry sleeping bag. The trick, of course, is actually having a warm bag and keeping it dry.

Down vs. Synthetic

Winter bags differ from three-season bags by having greater loft, or thickness, as well as a mummy design, a full hood, and a temperature rating below 5 degrees Fahrenheit. They're filled with either down or synthetic fiber for insulation. As with insulating clothing layers, the benefits of down-filled bags

Caring for Your Sleeping Bag

The old adage, "Take care of your equipment and it will take care of you," is important to live by in the winter, especially with gear as crucial as a sleeping bag. Dirt, sweat, and excess oils cause polyester and down fibers to clump, reducing a sleeping bag's loft and ability to insulate. Your bag rarely comes in contact with dirt while winter camping, so you shouldn't have to wash it very often. Just be sure to dry it completely before storing it. Never store your sleeping bag in the stuff sack provided with purchase, and never store it in a plastic bag. Instead, put it in a large cotton storage bag or pillowcase or, better yet, hang it in a closet. When you decide it's time for laundering, check the label for the manufacturer's instructions and follow them exactly. If the instructions differ from the following recommendations, follow the manufacturer's instructions—that way you won't jeopardize the bag's warranty.

Before washing, zip up all zippers, and then turn the bag inside out. Use front-loading washers, which are much gentler than top-loading washers. Avoid conventional detergents, bleaches, and fabric softeners, and use only a small amount of very mild soap that dissolves easily in water. Launder on a gentle cycle, and rinse the bag completely to remove all soapy residues. Once the bag is washed, roll it in several towels, gently press out the remaining water, and then either hang the bag to air dry or use a large commercial dryer on low heat to tumble dry. Do not dry clean sleeping bags, as the chemicals may damage them.

are numerous: they have the best warmth-to-weight ratio, they condense and pack down easily, take up little space in your pack, and last longer than synthetics when given proper care. However, down-filled bags cost significantly more than synthetic bags, they lose their ability to retain heat when wet, and take quite a bit longer to dry if they get wet.

Make your choice between the two insulating options based on the regions where you plan to camp and whether you think you'll take care of your bag. If you're a beginner or you think you might frequent wet climates, buy synthetic. If you opt for down, pay attention to the down fill you choose: 100 percent down fill, by regulation, contains nothing but down, but bags claiming to "contain" down may have up to 20 percent down fibers, not feathers. Also consider the loft, looking for bags that loft at least 550 cubic inches per ounce.

Mummy Bags

Sleeping bags are sold with various shapes, but only mummy bags retain enough heat to keep you warm during frigid winter nights. Mummy bags, because of their tapered shape, don't offer a lot of room to toss and turn. That snug fit traps heat effectively. They also compress well, facilitating packing. They come in various lengths, so be sure to get one that fits your body well, with a little extra space for a hot water bottle and damp clothing you plan to bring to bed with you. While the additional space offered by rectangular and semi-rectangular bags may be enticing, these bags are too heavy, they allow too much heat to escape, and their ability to compress is near negligible.

Temperature Rating

Pay attention to temperature rating and features when shopping for your perfect cocoon. A bag's temperature rating is set by its manufacturer (there's no industry standard) and will tell you approximately how low the temperature can be before the sleeping bag will no longer keep you warm. In general, bags with lower temperature ratings cost more. Choose a bag with a temperature rating at least ten degrees below the coldest temperature you anticipate. Look for a bag with an easy-to-find, easy-to-manipulate zipper and a Velcro tab covering the zipper closure. Your bag should have an insulated hood that fits snugly around your head and an insulated collar that wraps around your neck and cinches with its own drawstring. If the fill is synthetic, examine the bag's baffling and choose one with interior walls that overlap to prevent seams from being exposed to the cold. Lastly, but perhaps most importantly, compare the lofts of various bags. Lay your top choices side by side, allow each one a few minutes to expand, and see which has the greatest thickness.

Sleeping Pads

Our friend Halsey loves to tell the story about the time he took a group of middle school students on their first winter camping trip. In the middle of the first night, a student woke Halsey, saying that his tent mate was shaking uncontrollably and looked hypothermic. Halsey rushed to the student's side. The boy was shivering in his bag, and Halsey noticed that he'd failed to cinch his hood around his head and didn't fully close the top of his bag. Even worse, the boy had nothing between the bottom of his sleeping bag and the bottom of the tent—he was using his sleeping pad as a pillow.

The need for a sleeping pad (beneath your body, that is) boils down to this: when lying down, you'll crush the loft of your sleeping bag and lose that vital layer of protection between your body and the cold ground. Therefore, you need two pads to provide insulation—one full-length pad for the bottom half of your body and a one-half or three-quarter length pad for your torso. The shorter pad can protect your torso and head as you sleep and provide something to sit on when hanging around camp.

As with everything else, you can choose from different sleeping pad materials and sizes. You'll find three types of pads on the market—open-cell pads, closed-cell pads, and self-inflating pads—but only the latter two are acceptable for the backcountry. Open-cell pads are problematic because they soak up moisture and rip almost as easily as a piece of paper. Closed-cell foam pads are lightweight, affordable, durable, and don't absorb moisture. These sleeping pads are most dependable, but if you are more interested in comfort, use self-inflating pads such as those manufactured by Therm-a-Rest. (Of course, they don't fully self-inflate; you should let it inflate as much as possible, then blow in its valve to fully inflate the pad). Self-inflated pads compact very well when deflated and rolled, but because it's relatively easy to puncture them, make sure you have a repair kit and know how to use it. We've found the best plan is to carry one closed-cell foam pad and one self-inflating pad—each with different lengths.

Kitchenware

If you're an experienced three-season backcounty chef, you're likely equipped with nearly everything you will need in your winter kitchen. Perhaps the only additional item you'll want to buy is a metal stove base, which will prevent the heat from the stove from melting the nearby snow. You will also need more fuel in the winter than you need in the warmer months, especially if you will want nightly hot drinks (which you will) and plan to melt snow for drinking water (also highly probable). If you haven't yet amassed your backcounty kitchen or you're looking for a refresher about the different types of stoves and fuels, read on.

Stoves

It's imperative that you carry at least one stove on multiday trips. Hot food will fuel your warmth. Although you will be able to cook over open fires in some places (see Chapter 8), you can't rely on finding firewood everywhere you plan to camp, so a stove is a necessity. Your fuel source will determine your stove type, and we recommend white gas over all other fuels. Kerosene is a poor choice because it stinks, fails to produce much heat, and tends to coat everything in slimy grease. While butane lights quickly without priming and burns

Do not set your stove directly on the snow. Here, a lightweight metal stove base has been set on foot-long pieces of wood to keep the stove and pot from sinking into the snow.

To avoid stove setbacks, keep your stove clean and resist the urge to over-prime. If a hot stove's flame blows out in a gusty wind, it may be difficult to restart right away. Turn the stove off, let it cool, then try starting it again.

cleanly, it does so with much less heat and efficiency than white gas does when the temperature drops. White gas is superior because it burns hot and clean without producing much odor. It's also widely available in countries outside the United States, often under its chemical name, naphtha.

White gas burns in liquid-fuel stoves (also called white gas stoves), which require some setup and maintenance. To set up a liquid-fuel stove, have an experienced person demonstrate how to follow these steps (noting that different stoves have a slightly varied setup, so one should always consult the manual):

1. Expand the collapsed legs of the stove and set it on a flat, heat-resistant surface on top of the snow. If you choose not to purchase a lightweight metal stove base, you can create your own, using a piece of aluminum foil-covered wood or foam pad, or even an old license plate.
2. Pressurize the fuel by repeatedly pumping the fuel pump until it provides some resistance.
3. Attach the fuel canister to the stove via the stove's fuel line.
4. Prime the stove by opening the control valve until the priming cup fills with fuel halfway. Then turn the control valve off and light the priming fuel.
5. When the priming flame has diminished and nearly gone out, slowly open the control valve again.
6. If the stove goes out, turn the control valve off, let the stove cool, and repeat the priming process.

You should always clean and fire up your stove before setting out on a trip. Carry extra stove parts and a maintenance kit into the field and know how to disassemble and clean the fuel line and lubricate the O-ring. Learn how to clean the jet, too, though it's best to do this when you're home, away from the cold and the risk of dropping the jet into a snowy abyss.

Various liquid-stove models are on the market and newer, better ones hit the scene every year. Know the features you want and then consult with a gear retailer you trust. In general, you'll want an easy-to-use, durable stove with few parts that can crank out a significant amount of heat, but also has a simmering setting. It helps if useful accessories—such as a reflector, windscreen, pot grips, and a maintenance kit—are included with the stove. If not, you'll have to buy these items separately.

Pots and Utensils

Complete your kitchen with pots and utensils. For a group, it's best to have two large nesting pots—one for melting snow and boiling water for hot drinks and another for cooking meals. If you're on your own, one large pot will do (and make sure it's large, as it takes approximately 10 inches of snow to produce one inch of water). You'll need a snug lid for each pot and a pot grip. Kitchen utensils can include a ladle, a serving spoon, or both (depending on the menu) and individual bowls, spoons, and insulated mugs with lids. Mug lids and spoons are those often-used, easily losable items that you might consider securing. Using a leather awl, punch a hole in your mug lid, string a cord through the hole, and tie the string to the mug's handle. If you or your campmates are susceptible to losing spoons, everyone should create a spoon necklace by tying their spoon around their neck. It may seem a little silly, but the thought of eating hot soup with bare fingers in the cold of winter is enough to make spoon necklaces sound attractive.

To complete your kitchen wares, carry a small sponge and sump screen in a plastic bag—they'll come in handy when it's time to clean up. You can always bring a small bottle of biodegradable soap as well, but you won't necessarily need it, as snow is an excellent cleaning agent. Once a bowl or pot is mostly clean, add a dollop of snow and swoosh it around inside your bowl, using your spoon. Food particles will stick to the snow and freeze, coagulating into easy-to-clean clumps. To dispose of the clumps, cast them from the pot or bowl out over the snow. Disperse your diluted waste over a large area to avoid attracting animals.

Sporks

There's a spork for all seasons. Yes, a spoon is better than a fork when it comes to backcounty cutlery, but the utensil that combines them—the spork—is best. On chili nights (that is, nights when you have chili for dinner), you'll want a spoon, of course, but what about spaghetti nights? You can find affordable, durable, and heat-resistant sporks at specialty backpacking shops.

Repair Kits

Even if you take immaculate care of all your clothing and gear before, during, and after every trip, something is bound to fail. Fortunately, a well-stocked repair kit will give you the tools you need to fix most any gear-related problem you face. If we were to carry only one repair item, it would be duct tape. It can patch ripped tents and clothing, hold together busted sunglasses, and—if you're really resourceful and in a pinch—even be fashioned into everything from snowshoe straps to spoons. Along with packing a small roll, you should wrap a few strips of duct tape around ski poles so that you always have some tape readily available for quick fixes. Of course, we recommend carrying more than just duct tape, as it won't be too helpful if you need to repair your stove, and it's hardly the best tool for fixing a ski binding or replacing a shoelace.

A repair kit comes in handy on most winter hiking and camping trips. Here, a busted snowshoe has been repaired in the field using duct tape and lengths of extra nylon cord.

Your repair kit should include plenty of extra nylon cords of various thicknesses. Thinner cord can be used to replace shoelaces or help secure your shelter in heavy winds, while thicker cord can be used for lashing gear to your pack or even fixing a broken snowshoe. Also include flat webbing, cable ties, and large safety pins. A sewing kit is very useful and should include needles and threads of various thicknesses, along with a few straight pins and buttons. Dental floss is one of those great multipurpose items capable of doing more than picking jerky from between your teeth—it also serves as strong thread. Throw some glue or epoxy in your kit as well. Something like Super Glue works well for fixing everything from the frames of glasses to bindings, while Seam Grip adhesive is great for repairing seams.

Let your gear dictate which additional items to include in your repair kit. For example, if using a self-inflating sleeping pad, be sure you have patches appropriate for that material. If your pack buckles up with 1- and 2-inch clips, have a few of each along, and if your snowshoes' straps are removable and additional ones are available for purchase, do buy them. For your tent, carry a pole splint and a few swatches of adhesive Ripstop nylon.

Additional Clothing

When you plan to spend at least a night in the backcounty, your day clothes won't cut it—you need more layers. The clothing you take on day trips (as described in Chapter 4) will keep you warm when you're exercising and even during 20-minute rests, but it won't trap enough heat during extended periods of inactivity when you're lounging around camp. Camping wear adds insulation without redundancy and provides extra layers of hard-to-keep-dry items such as gloves and socks.

In general, you'll want at least one additional insulating layer; it should be a very puffy down or synthetic parka that you can layer over everything else. You might also consider puffy synthetic pants. Ever since we invested in big down jackets with insulated pockets and spent the cash on synthetic pants, we've found winter camping much more enjoyable. When one of us announces, "Time for da pants!" it's a sign that the day's activities are over and it's time to relax. We complete our outfits with camp booties, which come with either synthetic or down and have stiff soles to allow short walks around camp.

We try to avoid redundant layers unless we're certain we'll need them. We almost never carry more than one set of base layers (long underwear) because these tend to stay dry or at least dry quickly. We do, however, carry additional accessories. We have a little stuff sack full of different headwear, including ear bands, beanies, and thick ski caps. We carry an extra pair of liner gloves—these almost always get wet—and an extra pair of mittens. We also carry a few extra pairs of socks and each keep one thick, warm pair in the bottom of our sleeping bag to wear only at night.

Personal Gear

Just one day before our group was scheduled to leave the backcountry after a two-week expedition, our friend Jacki pulled out her secret weapon—moisturized towelettes. We'd all noticed how Jacki's skin seemed to glow while the rest of our hands and faces withered into chapped, red raisins, but we thought she was just naturally blessed with moisturized skin. No, she assured us, it was all because of the towelettes. She'd learned at a young age never to leave home without them, even if it meant carrying extra weight on her back. Once she confessed her little luxury, one group member mentioned his blow-up pillow and another said she knew it was crazy, but she always carried her pet rock that had brought her luck and kept her safe since childhood.

Although you most likely won't have such a smattering of random items that you *just can't live without*, you might have a little thing that doesn't weigh much, brings you great comfort, and is fine to bring with you into the backcountry. You'll also have the standard personal toiletry items such as a toothbrush, toothpaste, corrective eye wear, and sunscreen. If traveling with a group, you can opt for sharing tubes of toothpaste and sunscreen. But leave the deodorant, shampoo, conditioner, and lotions at home—unless, of course, you *just can't live without them*, they're biodegradable, and you promise not to complain about the extra weight.

Children's Camping Gear

Every reputable backcountry camping outfitter will carry children's camping gear. In general, kids' gear is very similar to adults'—only smaller. Look for the same types of features in children's sleeping bags and clothing as you do with adult gear. However, if a child won't be carrying a lot of weight, it isn't important that he or she have the highest quality backpack on the market. Children may be able to carry their sleeping bags, clothes, some water, and snacks, but they shouldn't be asked to carry heavy items such as food or a tent until adolescence. The general rule is that people should carry less than one-fifth of their body weight on their back. For a 60-pound child, that means the packed backpack should weigh no more than 12 pounds.

It's best that small children on camping trips sleep in tents, as opposed to sleeping under a tarp. Tents symbolize home and security, which is especially important in an unfamiliar environment. There is no specific kid-friendly feature you need to look for when shopping for a tent, but you might consider making the tent more home-like and cozy by outfitting it with your child's favorite blanket or stuffed animal.

CHAPTER EIGHT

In Camp

After a long day on the trail, we welcome the thought of a hot drink, a belly full of warm food, and a good night's sleep. Of course, all these things are available back at home, so we could easily head to the car and drive back into civilization. But the winter camp has such strong allure! Out in the elements on a cold winter night, it's possible to enjoy an outdoor experience more beautiful and serene than anything you would find at any other time of year. When long afternoon shadows begin to creep across the trail and you feel your muscles begin to ache with the day's exertion, it's time to start thinking about setting up camp. Consult your map, choose an area to scout for a campsite, and head toward it. Slow your pace during the final fifteen minutes or so—your body will benefit from the cool-down.

Site Selection

Finding the ideal campsite—or making one—is much easier in the winter than during other seasons. The snow softens nature's edges, covering jagged boulders and stumps that might get in sleep's way in warmer seasons. Where flat land is scarce, snow can be shaped into a mound and leveled off to form a perfect tent platform. And you don't need to worry about setting up camp near a fresh water source—all that snow can provide as much drinking water as you desire. That said, you still need to be mindful about where you plan to make your home for the night, and that takes some advance planning. Before you begin your trip, learn the rules and regulations about camping in a specific area. Within just a few miles, some areas may be open to camping and others not, often because you will travel back and forth between public and private property. While land management agencies generally relax their camping regulations in the

In this Maine Woods camp, campers created a tent platform by stomping out a flat surface in the snow. They then dug down into the snow in front of the tent door to create a "mudroom" where they could take off their boots before entering their shelter.

winter—it's hard to enforce the "camp in designated sites only" rule when sites are covered with snow—some lands do have specific camping areas year-round, or prohibit camping altogether. Knowing the rules and following them could save you from being fined and could potentially save your life. Backcountry rules are put in place for a reason, and it's usually to protect human safety, the environment, or both. In the backcountry, you should consult a map after lunch, find a few potential camping spots that look promising, and determine whether or not they meet your criteria for a great site. Once you've reached the area you are considering for a campsite, have everyone drop their packs and scout out the area, asking themselves the following questions as they go:

Is this site protected from avalanches, high winds, and other environmental hazards? Setting up camp at the base of an avalanche-prone slope is about the dumbest thing someone could do in the backcountry, but it happens more often than you'd like to think. Know how to evaluate avalanche conditions and avoid putting yourself in the thick of a big slide (see Chapter 10). Stay away from cliff edges that someone may slip from in the middle of the night and refrain from camping below a dead tree or a widow-maker (a tree or large branch that's already toppled but precariously hangs in another tree's branches). Imagine the conditions at the site if the wind were to whip violently or if the clouds opened up and dropped heaps of snow. Unless you're absolutely sure you're in for a calm night (or you have the experience and gear to handle a really rough one), avoid the temptation to camp on an exposed ridge. Sure, the view may be spectacular, but safety comes first.

Does this site maximize warm air and sunlight? Camping at the lowest point in a valley—the point where cold air settles for the night—is almost as silly (and potentially dangerous) as camping atop a peak. Your warmest option is to camp atop a sheltered knoll facing south, which situates you to take advantage of the day's light. If possible, select a site with no obstructions to the east.

Is a water source nearby? If you have ample fuel for melting snow, it's not necessary to have a water source other than snow. However, you will save loads of time and fuel if you can access water near your campsite. See Chapter 9 for more information about accessing and treating water in the backcountry.

Is firewood plentiful? This is relevant only if you plan to make a fire and know you can do so with minimal impact (see Chapter 1). Scout the area around your campsite for dry, dead, and downed branches no wider in diameter than your wrist. It's preferable that the wood be bark-free so that it has less moisture (which gets trapped between the wood and bark).

Will it be easy to minimize impact at this site? People often incorrectly assume that the Leave No Trace principles (see Chapter 1) can be ignored when a blanket of snow separates humans from the bare ground. However, water sources are still vulnerable to pollution, as is the rest of the environment. Set up camp at least 200 feet away from springs, streams, lakes, and other bodies of water. Don't camp directly on the trail, even though it's covered in snow. Other hikers won't enjoy untangling themselves from your tent's guy lines or skiing over your designated pee spot.

While the view is not imperative to a good campsite, you may want to scope it out. Some people find this to be more important than others, but we think it's definitely worth the effort to find the most scenic spot around. After all, you worked so hard to make it to your campsite, you might as well enjoy the view! You'll enjoy it all the more after you've set up a well-organized camp that will provide you a comfortable home base in even the most challenging winter conditions.

Making Camp

We've never been the kind of people to redecorate our house with luxury wares (or had the money to be those kind of people), but once in the wintry back-country, our inner feng shui masters emerge. We obsessively craft elaborate kitchens, complete with carved benches and cabinetry, and build garages and bathrooms (see figure 8.1). We grade our tent site for the optimal sleeping angle and, after pitching our fly so taut that you could bounce a coin off it, we dig out a mudroom near the vestibule and park our skis in the garage next door. It may sound over-the-top, but approaching camp setup as though we were master carpenters creating the home of our dreams helps us stay organized.

We've become efficient at making camp over the years, but every time we head out with less-experienced travelers, we're reminded how long it takes to do all the required tasks before truly relaxing for the night. With a group, it's easy to divide tasks and have everyone start their work as soon as you have agreed where you'll set up the various parts of camp. Although some tasks (such as collecting firewood) require more effort than others, everyone should be aware that the day's aerobic activities mostly end once a site is selected. It's a good idea to layer up as soon as the pack is off your back. But don't take off your skis or snowshoes just yet, particularly if the snow is deep—you'll need them to stomp out an even, compacted surface so you don't post hole around camp.

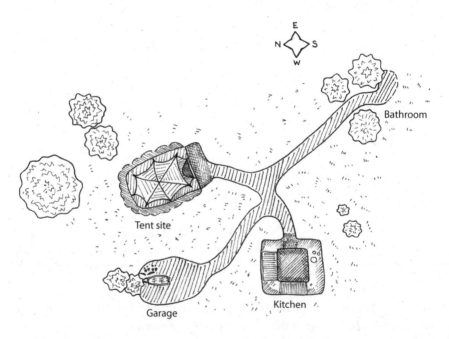

Fig. 8.1. With a little ingenuity, you can create an outdoor home such as the one illustrated here.

As soon as you reach camp, put on an extra layer or two to avoid losing all the heat you've built up on the trail. If it's really cold, put on your big puffy parka—there's nothing warmer!

While someone fires up the stove to melt snow (or, if a water source is close, to boil water for hot drinks), others can divide the following tasks: setting up shelter, collecting firewood, creating a kitchen and living area, and prepping for dinner. Setting up shelter is the top priority. Start by selecting your tent site within the camp, avoiding widow-makers and other potentially hazardous features. The tent site should be protected from the wind while open to as much morning sunlight as possible.

The Tent Site

Once you've found the perfect tent site, stomp out an area about twice as large as the tent's footprint. To create a flat surface, walk back and forth and in circles while wearing snowshoes, skis, or a split board. Even then, it may take up to

A windbreak wall of snow around your tent—or around multiple tents, as shown at this tent compound in the Andes (Chile)—is priceless when the wind blows hard.

an hour for the snow to set, depending on its condition. If you're working with really dry powder and have to let it sit a bit before setting a tent on it, busy yourself with other camp chores—there's plenty to do, including stomping out paths between the tent site, the kitchen/living area, and a designated pee tree. Creating paths is helpful because you will be able to take off your snowshoes or skis once the snow sets and you won't have to put them on again until you hit the trail the following day.

The next step in camp creation is the digging of a mudroom in front of where the tent door will be. A mudroom, a rectangular pit before the tent's entrance, makes it easy to sit comfortably at the tent's edge with your legs bent while you eat or change out of your heavy boots and into those cozy camp booties you've been looking forward to putting on. To make a mudroom, directly in front of where the tent door will open, cut down a foot or two with your snow shovel and then shovel snow out and away from the door.

Building a windbreak wall on the upwind side of the tent is always a good idea, but pitch the tent first so that you can build the wall as close to it as possible without the two touching. If you have the time and energy—and especially if you expect high or shifting winds through the night—build the wall to surround most of the tent. Moisture-laden snow works best when creating walls, as you can cut snow blocks and quickly stack those on top of one another. If you're

The best windbreak walls are created from snow blocks stacked one on top of the other.

anticipating extremely severe winds, dig down a few feet into the snow before stomping out the tent platform and creating the wall. This is the same technique you would employ if you were camping under a tarp shelter (see Chapter 7).

The Bathroom

Once the platform settles and you've pitched the tent, you'll be ready to move on to the other "rooms," including the bathroom, garage, kitchen, and dining area. The bathroom is merely a designated area away from camp where people can go to do their business. It isn't necessary for everyone to urinate in the same area, but it does save your campsite from multiple unbecoming splotches and it eliminates the possibility that pee-soaked snow will be melted for drinking water. When it comes to defecating, everyone should adhere to the third Leave No Trace principle, which concerns proper waste disposal (see Chapter 1).

Young people are particularly sensitive about bathroom issues and nervous about their peers potentially stumbling upon them. To avoid this, you can hang a bright bandana in a tree on the way to the designated spot—when people go to the bathroom they can take the bandana with them so others know the pee tree is occupied.

The Garage

The garage is the gear storage area of camp. In a designated spot, park your pulk or sled. Pile food bags one on top of the other. Place your group repair kit, first-aid kit, and any loose maps and compasses together in the top food bag so they're easily accessible. Stick snowshoes, skis, shovels, and ice axes vertically into the snow so that they stand out, even if heavy snow falls through the night. Make sure everything is grouped together and nothing will blow away in the night.

The Kitchen

Creativity flourishes when constructing a kitchen and dining area. Before digging in, take a moment to think about where the bench should be, where to place the counter, and where you plan to cook. If you plan to have a fire—and especially if you plan to cook over it—you'll need the area to be larger than it

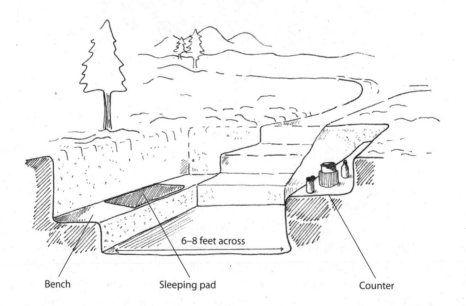

6–8 feet across

Bench   Sleeping pad   Counter

Fig. 8.2. You can construct a kitchen, similar to the one illustrated here, when setting up camp.

would be if you're cooking over a stove. Consider facing the kitchen eastward in order to catch the maximum morning sun. For a group of four to six people, make the pit about 6 to 8 feet in diameter. While you're digging out the inside of the pit with your snow shovel, pile the snow on the outside edges in order to create a bench. The bench should eventually be wide enough to accommodate a sleeping pad (laid horizontally) and high enough so people sitting on it can dangle their feet above the cold ground. To make a plush bench, you can pack the snow with a shovel, then scoop out seats and assemble backrests using skis or snowshoes. Opposite the bench, sculpt the piled snow into a kitchen counter. Adorn the counter with anything you like, from cubbyholes for food storage to a plastic-lined pit for collecting garbage. As you become an experienced craftsperson, you'll find yourself tweaking your design to maximize your comfort, adding features such as carved out toe space beneath the counter so you don't have to stand duck-footed while cooking (see figure 8.2).

Securing the Shelter

While winter and summer camping have many things in common, securing a tent is not one of them. In summer, you can often simply throw your sleeping pad and bag inside a pitched tent and consider it secure without even tying down the guy lines. When you do secure your tent in warmer seasons, you can rely on those flimsy stakes that are included with your tent or count on finding a plethora of rocks scattered around the bare ground to use as anchors. In winter, however, it's imperative that you *always* secure the tent and recognize that rocks will be covered in snow and that three-season tent stakes won't give you the purchase you need—instead, buy some thick snow stakes and learn how to create deadman anchors.

The first trick to securing a tent is to pitch it as tautly as possible. This is particularly important because snow loads and high winds can put immense pressure on a tent's fabric if it's not stretched tightly over its frame. In fierce winds a few people will need to work together to set up the tent and ensure it doesn't blow away in the process. Follow these steps before sliding the poles through their loops: while one person holds the tent flat to the ground, others should stake out the corners of the tent and attach the poles. Repeat the process with the fly.

Many options are available for anchoring tents in winter, and you'll often employ all of them simultaneously. You may wind up securing one corner with a buried stuff sack, another with a snow stake or partially buried ski, and still

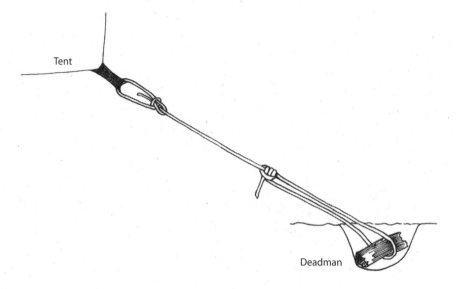

Tent

Deadman

Fig. 8.3. Burying a deadman in the snow is an excellent way to anchor your tent.

another with a deadman (see figure 8.3). A deadman is anything used as a weight and buried in the snow to act as an anchor. Deadmen are often sticks, though they can be rocks, snow-filled stuff sacks, or even stakes lying horizontally. To use a deadman, follow these steps:

1. Dig a hole that is at least 6 inches deep and about 12 inches wide (depending on the size of the object you are using as a deadman) at a 45-degree angle to the tent's corner and about 3 feet from the tent.
2. String your guy or stake line out from the tent, into the hole, and back out the hole away from the tent.
3. Wrap the guy or stake line around the deadman and place it in the hole.
4. Tie a taut-line hitch (preferably far enough from the deadman that it will be accessible above the snow, once snow is filled in over the anchor).
5. Fill the hole with snow and compress it around the anchor by stomping on it.
6. Let the snow set.
7. Tighten the guy or stake lines by adjusting the hitches.

Deadmen make fantastic anchors, but beware that snow usually freezes around them through the night, making them very difficult to remove in the morning. If your anchor is an inorganic substance (such as a stake or stuff sack) be sure you have a shovel handy in the morning to remove it. You can also tie lines off to partially buried snowshoes, skis, or split boards, as long as you're sure you won't need the gear again until it's time to break down the tent. If you've opted for tarp camping over tent camping, you can still employ the same techniques for anchoring your shelter.

Cooking

It may seem counterintuitive, but the key to cooking is getting the hot drinks going as soon as possible! Even if your dinner turns into a soggy flop, you'll go to bed happy when you're well hydrated with warm liquids. While a few people are working on camp setup, the cooks should busy themselves finding a water source (see Chapter 9) and heating water for beverages. When heating water and cooking over a stove, place the stove on a platform to prevent it from sinking into a white abyss, and employ a windscreen, a heat reflector, and a pot lid, all of which increase a stove's efficiency (see Chapter 7). Even if you plan to cook dinner over a fire, get the backup stove cranking for hot drinks while others are collecting wood and building the fire.

There are a few tricks for cooking in fierce weather. Efficiency is key, which is why we recommend one-pot meals and strong stove skills. Familiarize yourself with your stove long before setting out on a winter trip, and practice turning it on and operating it while wearing a pair of thin gloves. You may be tempted to retreat into your tent and cook in the vestibule, but this is widely discouraged; it increases condensation in the tent and could possibly lead to asphyxiation. If the weather is so poor that you feel you must cook in the vestibule, be careful. Light the stove only if you're sure you can prevent it from flaring, keep flammable items (such as polypro and other fabrics) away, and properly ventilate your vestibule and tent. Never, ever, cook inside the tent itself.

Campfires

It's been said that fire is the rose of winter. With its warm glow and enticing heat, fire is usually a welcome sight in the winter camp, but not always. Because many campers have abused their right to build fires in the backcountry—charring the bare ground and leaving a soiled trail of burned foil and garbage—fires are no longer allowed in some areas. Where fires are permitted, you can enjoy them and use them for cooking while minimizing their impact. There is a certain mystique about cooking over a wood fire (and what's camping without a little smoke in your eyes?). Everyone should have the opportunity to cook over a campfire at some point in their lives and doing so during the winter can be quite special. To prepare a fire pit in the snow and create a hot, efficient, and clean-burning fire that leaves no trace, follow these steps:

1. *Start by collecting tinder*, the smallest and driest fire-starting material you can find. This may be dry birch bark, dead pine needles, or matchstick-thin twigs collected from blow-downs. We often keep a plastic bag in a pocket of our shell jacket as we hike and occasionally fill it with tinder that we find near the trail. This gives us a little something to do while we're hiking and, by collecting tinder as we go, it means we have one fewer task to complete when we get into camp. Once you've collected the tinder, pile it up in camp near the site where you will eventually build the fire pit.

2. *Collect kindling* (finger-size twigs and sticks that feed a growing flame after the tinder is lit), which is often found near the trunks of evergreens. After you've collected kindling in an assortment of sizes, create a pile next to the pile of tinder.

3. *Collect firewood*. Look for dead, downed, or leaning branches approximately the size of your wrist. These will serve as your firewood. Dry wood without bark burns best, and you should look for hard woods such as ash, beech, and oak. Birch does not make good firewood, so it should be avoided. The amount of wood you collect depends on how long you expect your fire to burn and whether you plan to cook over it, as fires for cooking must burn hotter (with more wood) than fires that merely provide light and warmth. When you've collected the amount that will suffice for your needs, pile it next to the mound of kindling.

4. *Dig a fire pit* in the middle of your kitchen area. It should be 1 to 2 feet deep at a diameter of about 10 inches. Surround the perimeter of your pit with fist-size rocks (if available) to delineate the fire ring.

5. *Create a fire foundation* because without a platform, your fire will either sink into the snow as it burns, eventually putting itself out with the snow it melts into, or it will burn to the ground, scorching and scarring the bare earth. All you need for a platform are a series of branches or logs, or one thick layer of rotten wood placed at the base of the pit.

6. *Get the fire started*. Place a handful of tinder on the platform and lean three of the smallest pieces of kindling against it so they form a teepee around the tinder. Light the tinder with either a strike-anywhere match (which you've kept dry in a waterproof container) or a lighter. If the temperature is so cold that your lighter won't light, warm it for a minute against your skin or under your armpit and try lighting it again. Once the tinder is burning, slowly add additional pieces of kindling to the teepee. Remember that fire needs air to

burn; maintain air spaces between the kindling sticks to avoid smothering the flames. When the kindling is burning well, surround the teepee with a square of firewood. The firewood will eventually start to burn, at which point you should add additional pieces, continuing to arrange them in a square formation (similar to a basic log cabin).

7. *Keep the fire going.* Fan the flame and add additional wood as needed, being careful not to build the fire larger than the pit.

If you plan to cook over the fire, you'll need to create a tripod from which to hang a chain and attach your cooking pot. This cooking method requires three long branches, a chain (which you can purchase at an outdoor store) and a hook. Look for three pieces of live wood (dead wood will burn) that are approximately 5 feet long, stick one end of each branch in the snow, and angle the

Small fires provide warmth and light, as well as a heat source to cook over.

pieces so that they meet each other directly above the fire. Secure the ends of the branches together with the chain and let the end of the chain dangle over the fire. Hook the handle of your pot to the chain so that the bottom of the pot hangs directly over the fire's flame. You can adjust the distance between the flame and the pot, depending on the amount of heat needed to cook whatever is in the pot.

Whether enjoying a fire as a fuel source for cooking or simply as a source for light and heat, be sure that you put it out completely before going to bed (see Chapter 1).

Snow Shelters

When we led a group of teenage boys out on a multiday winter camping trip in northern Maine, one boy named Adam stood out, though he was at least a foot shorter than the next shortest boy. His energy and enthusiasm were astounding, and what he lacked in stature he more than made up for in confidence. When it was time for overnight solos, we realized that we were one tarp short of giving each group member his own shelter. Adam quickly piped up that he would go without—he knew how to build a quinzhee, a hollowed-out pile of snow, and would prefer one anyway. We shook our heads in amusement, handed over the shovel, and sent him on his way.

When we returned to check on the boys an hour later, each of them had erected his tarp, gathered his pile of firewood, and then sat near his shelter looking bored. Adam, on the other hand, was still furiously working on the finishing touches of his quinzhee, smoothing out the domed ceiling and adding a chimney for ventilation. He gave us an enthusiastic thumbs-up sign, grinned ear-to-ear, and waved us on.

That night a storm raged and we worried about the boys. Without their knowing, we snuck around to ensure that their tarps were still standing and that none of them were signaling for help. Many tarps sagged and more than once we had to help a boy tighten his guy lines and revise his anchor system. But Adam's shelter looked strong, and he was nowhere in sight.

After a fitful night's sleep, morning came. We trudged through the freshly fallen snow to pick up the boys, all of whom were waiting wide-eyed by the trail, eager to reunite with their peers and share their harrowing tale of braving it through the storm. But when we came upon Adam's camp, he wasn't there. We called his name but heard no response. We pulled away the backpack that was blocking his shelter's entrance, peeked our heads into his quinzhee, and found him lying there, still sleeping. When we finally roused him, he sat up, rubbed his eyes, and exclaimed he'd just enjoyed the best night's sleep of his life. From inside his warm, cozy quinzhee, he'd had no idea that a storm raged outside.

People like Adam choose snow shelters over tents and tarps because they're fun to build and once they're finished, they can be touched up with custom features. Snow shelters are warm, block wind better than tents do, and can be built in an open area. In an emergency situation, knowing how to build a snow shelter can also save your life. (Plus, they're always good for tiring out ambitious boys like Adam.) They do require a lot of time and energy to build, and setting up a tent or a tarp is much easier. That said, we encourage everyone to give snow shelters a try.

Just as the number of Inuit words for snow is myriad, there are countless different snow shelter designs in the world. We'll discuss the two designs most widely used in the continental United States, as shelters such as igloos require slab snow that isn't commonly found where you're likely to go camping. Snow caves and quinzhees, the shelters we'll discuss here, are both hollowed-out piles of snow, but there's a difference: with snow caves, you find a large drift of snow and hollow it out; with quinzhees, you find fallen snow, pile it together into a large mound, and then hollow it out. Where deep drifts are plentiful, a snow cave is your best bet because you'll save the arduous step of first having to create the pile of snow. Quinzhees, on the other hand, are advantageous when deep drifts aren't available because you can build them anywhere you find a few feet of loose snow.

Whether building a snow cave or a quinzhee, keep in mind that smaller shelters are inherently stronger than bigger ones. If you're with a large group, it's best to craft multiple shelters, each for three or four people. Also recognize the potential of a structure collapsing during its construction. While someone excavates from the inside, another person outside the shelter should be prepared to dig, should a collapse occur. Also beware of snow conditions. If snow is either too wet and sloppy or too powdery and unconsolidated, the shelter is likely to be unstable. Don't bother trying to build a snow shelter and opt for a tent or tarp if the snow is very wet. If the snow is very dry, however, you just need to allow time for the snow to settle after construction and before entering the shelter. The optimal snow for snow shelters is found in consolidated drifts—this snow holds enough moisture to settle well, but is dry enough to ensure that the structure will be solid.

Snow Caves

Site selection is the first step to erecting a snow cave. Look for snowdrifts at least 6 feet high on the leeward side (facing away from the prevailing wind) of

Excavating out snow shelters is wet work, so you'll want to wear your waterproof shell. It can also be very aerobic work, which you'll need to keep in mind to avoid overheating. You'll often be on your knees while digging, so place a closed-cell insulated pad beneath you. Rotate out with a partner or two so that you each take turns digging.

downed trees, boulders, ridges, and stream banks. Scout out areas downwind of open spaces where snow tends to accumulate. When you've found what you think is a good drift, check to be sure you're out of avalanche terrain and then use a ski pole to probe the mound, making sure it's deep enough and not riddled with boulders or fallen logs that will impede your digging.

After you've selected the right drift, it's time to start digging. First dig straight into the leeward slope. Once the entrance is at least a foot deep, start angling it upward. Eventually you'll want a tunnel that is about 3 feet high, wide, and deep, with its top lower than the sleeping area's base. This last point is important because warm air must be trapped in the sleeping area, while cold air (which sinks) must have an escape route.

The next step entails digging out the main chamber so that it can accommodate your group (generally no more than four people) sleeping under a domed ceiling. The ceiling and walls should eventually be 12 to 18 inches thick. If there are plentiful sticks around the outside of your shelter, get a dozen of them, break them into foot-long lengths, and plunge them into the shelter from the outside at various points. That way the diggers will know they've excavated enough when they hit the inner edges of the sticks. When the sticks are removed, perfect little ventilation holes remain. If sticks aren't an option, diggers should keep their eyes out for blue light. Blue light indicates that a wall is 12 to 18 inches thick. In order to see the blue light, however, you often need to block the light coming in through the main entrance. At that point you might see areas that are brighter (more yellowish-white than blue), indicating areas that are too thin and require additional layers of snow to "patch" them up and make them thicker.

Once you are finished with basic construction, make sure you have proper ventilation. You should be fine if you have a bunch of tiny holes (left by the extracted sticks), but another option is to punch one fist-size hole through the middle of the ceiling (see figure 8.4). Check your ventilation hole(s) occasionally

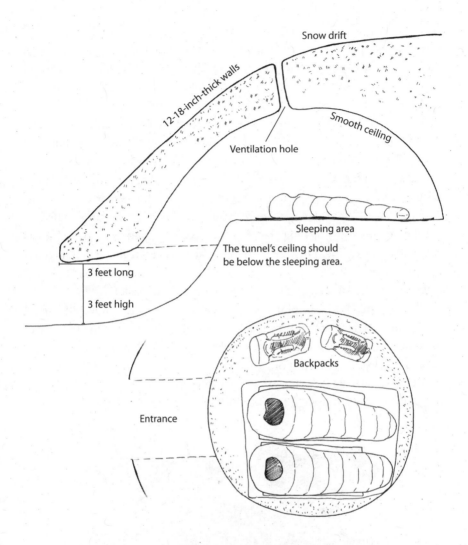

Snow drift

12-18-inch-thick walls

Smooth ceiling

Ventilation hole

Sleeping area

3 feet long

The tunnel's ceiling should
be below the sleeping area.

3 feet high

Backpacks

Entrance

Fig. 8.4. A snow cave can provide a warm, cozy place for a winter camper to sleep.

to ensure that they haven't filled in with snow. You should also smooth out your ceiling, thus ensuring that melting snow will slide down the walls instead of dripping on your sleeping bag. Place your skis or snowshoes at the shelter's entrance to mark your home so you know where to find it. Bring a shovel inside with you, in case you need to dig yourself out. Before pulling out the sleeping bags, lay a ground tarp or emergency blanket down, then the sleeping pads, and lastly the bags. For a final touch, light a candle and watch its light dance across the room.

Quinzhees

All the above applies to a quinzhee, too, but site selection is different. Instead of finding a snowdrift to dig into, you get to make one! All you need is snow and a shovel. In an emergency situation when you don't have the shovel, you can always use your snowshoe, a pot lid, or even your gloved hands.

For a quinzhee to accommodate two or three people, it should have a diameter of about 7 feet. Place a ski on the ground and use that to measure out your circle. Then walk the circle's perimeter a few times to harden the snow. Compacted snow at the periphery works best because it will become the foundation for your walls. However, don't compact the snow in the center of the circle, because that will make more work for yourself when it comes time to hollow out the pile for your sleeping chamber. Instead, pile tightly sealed backpacks and stuff sacks on the inner circle so that easy space is created when it comes time to excavate. In the center of the circle, place a long, thin pole. The pole will eventually alert the diggers to the midpoint of the shelter.

The next step is to start piling on the snow. Eventually the snow pile should reach at least 6 feet high at its center. Pack down the snow with the flat side of the shovel, add more snow, and repeat the process until you have a solid mound. It may need to set for an hour or so before it's firm enough to withstand excavation. Once ready, dig it out the same way you would a snow cave, taking care to make the entrance way slightly lower than the main area (see figure 8.5).

This little boy enjoys going in and out of the quinzhee his parents have built near their home in Concord, New Hampshire.

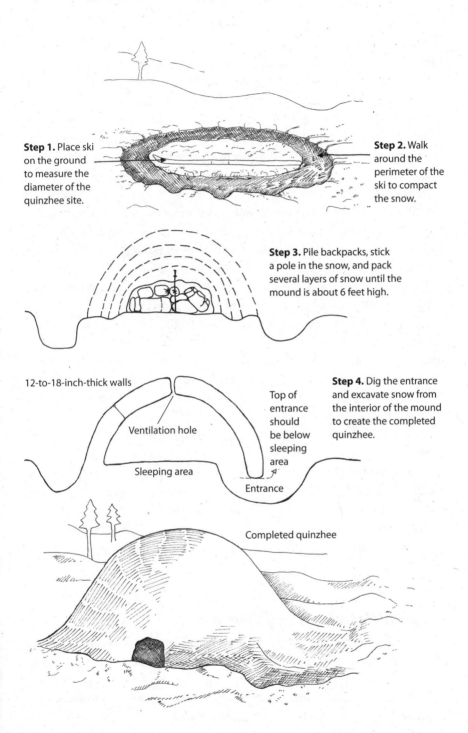

Step 1. Place ski on the ground to measure the diameter of the quinzhee site.

Step 2. Walk around the perimeter of the ski to compact the snow.

Step 3. Pile backpacks, stick a pole in the snow, and pack several layers of snow until the mound is about 6 feet high.

12-to-18-inch-thick walls

Ventilation hole

Sleeping area

Top of entrance should be below sleeping area

Entrance

Step 4. Dig the entrance and excavate snow from the interior of the mound to create the completed quinzhee.

Completed quinzhee

Fig. 8.5. Like a snow cave, a quinzhee is a great alternative to a tent. Follow the steps to build your own quinzhee.

Kids in Camp

Children usually delight in the adventure of camping out in the snow. Not all camp chores are kid-friendly, but every child can pitch in one way or another. Toddlers need constant attention in camp, and they can assist with setup by gathering sticks and by handing mom or dad small items such as snow stakes or kitchen utensils. Preschoolers can do all that and help with spreading out sleeping bags and pads and building the fire ring with stones. Children between the ages of 6 and 8 make great assistant chefs (as long as they stay away from the stove and fire). They usually like the challenge of trying to get a sleeping bag into its stuff sack. If you run out of necessary camp jobs to delegate to children, you can always engage kids by having them contribute to the group journal. Kids are great at describing the day's adventures in writing or with drawings, so consider packing along a few markers and a small journal.

Whether or not kids can help out around camp, they should always wear a whistle for safety and learn the secrets of staying found (see Chapter 6). Older children (ages 8 and up) can do most anything around camp, but they still need supervision with stoves and fire. If you plan to build a fire in a camp that children inhabit, take extra precautions. Mandate a "hands- and sticks-off" policy and be sure that the fire is constantly monitored by an adult. Some older, more mature children can be trusted to help tend a fire, but this can become tricky if you allow some kids to help while others aren't allowed.

The time between dinner and sleeping can be full of anxiety for some kids. Children are used to their nightly routine, so they need some of home's comforts. When camping with small children, bring along their favorite blanket or picture book. Older children may revel in the excitement of winter camping and may want to stay up late, roast s'mores over the fire, and tell ghost stories. As long as you're sure they will get enough sleep to be energized the next morning, go ahead and indulge these kids' desires. After all, winter camping should be fun!

Staying Warm and Dry Overnight

You can afford to be cold and wet during the day, but only if you can get warm and dry at night and stay that way until morning. When we met in Patagonia, Chile, our feet were cold and wet every single day. But for at least eight hours a night, they were warm and toasty, so they—and we—were all right. Staying warm and dry overnight takes a little more awareness than you might think. Here we share our time-tested nightly sequence to ensure that you wake up warm and refreshed:

- After dinner, enjoy a hot drink while you boil water for your water bottle. Once you fill your bottle with hot water, stuff it in the bottom of your sleeping bag so that it will add warmth to your bag before you even settle into it for the night. Depending on the thickness of your bag and insulating pad, the water may stay warm until morning, providing you with a little foot heater through the night.
- If you've built a fire, dry your wet clothing out around the fire, being sure to keep materials from burning. Extinguish the fire properly (see Chapter 1).
- Take a sweep through camp to make sure everything is secure and in its proper place, then tighten down the tent's guy lines so you don't have to get out and do it in the middle of the night.
- If traveling in bear country during a time that you suspect bear activity, tie a sack full of all your food up in a tree.
- Brush your teeth and go to the bathroom.
- Before getting inside the tent, brush any excess snow off your clothes. Sit at the tent's entrance, take your gaiters and boots off, and brush the snow off of them.
- Fold the gaiter over the top of the boot, put the boot on its side, and then slide the top of the boot under your sleeping pad near where your hips will be. This way, your boots won't freeze during the night and you will have an easier time staying put on your pad. Alternatively, you can put your boots and gaiters in a stuff sack and then put that in between your legs in your sleeping bag.
- Climb into the tent and close the door.
- Strip down to your long underwear and hat. If you tend to sleep cold, add a thin insulating top over your long underwear top, but avoid the temptation to go to bed wearing everything you own. If your clothes are wet, exchange them for dry ones and then bring the wet ones to bed with you.
- Take off your socks and place them against your skin on your thighs, even if they're wet. This will warm them for the morning, when it's time to put them back on.
- Let your feet air dry for a few minutes while you do a few sit-ups to generate body heat.
- Put on the pair of dry socks you've been storing in the base of your sleeping bag. If your feet tend to get cold, wrap a sweater around them or sleep in your insulated booties.
- Put extra outer layers between your sleeping bag and sleeping pad.
- Crawl into your bag, bringing along additional clothing layers and water bottles to fill some of the dead air spaces. Some dead air space is good—

when heated by your body, it provides pockets of warm air all around you. But there often exists more dead air in a bag than you'll be able to warm with your body alone, so it's a good idea to fill some of that space with clothing. We recommend putting one or two garments into your bag with you.

- Put extra clothing into a stuff sack and arrange that under your head like a pillow.
- Near your head, place your headlamp and some extra food and water. You'll want the headlamp if you need to get out during the night, and the food will come in handy if you wake up cold in the middle of the night and need a calorie jolt to boost your internal furnace.
- Utilize your sleeping bag to its fullest, cinching the hood around your head, closing the insulated sleeve around your neck, and zipping the side

Hang your sleeping bags over a line and allow them to dry in the morning sun before packing them into the stuff sacks.

zip completely closed. With all this tightening down, you should still have your mouth and nose outside of the bag to reduce moisture build-up and facilitate breathing.

■ Rest and go to sleep.

Eventually you'll wake and it may not yet be morning. If you're new at winter camping, it's quite common to wake up multiple times as your body adjusts to the experience. With so many hours in the tent, you'll probably need to urinate at some point. Do it! Avoid the temptation to wait it out. One of the most difficult things to convince yourself is that you should get up and go to the bathroom in the middle of the night when it's freezing out there. If you hold it, however, your body will waste precious energy keeping all that fluid warm. Plus, you won't be able to get back to sleep. If you take a moment to rush outside and relieve yourself, you'll be surprised by how little warmth you lose in the process and how quickly you manage to fall back to sleep.

Seize the Day!

Mornings are especially brilliant in the winter, when sun lights the snow and brings along a welcome dose of warmth. Since daylight hours are so few in the winter, it's important that you take full advantage of them and get the day started with the sun. As soon as you wake, do a few sit-ups in bed to generate a little body heat before parting with your bag. Then dress quickly, trapping as much of that heat as possible. If the sun is shining, loop your sleeping bag over a tree so it can dry in the light before you pack it up. If there's no wind, turn the tent on its side so the moisture on its bottom can evaporate. Get hot drinks going as soon as possible. Once breakfast is on and camp is packed up, it's time to check the map, make a goal, and hit the trail!

CHAPTER NINE
Food and Water

The belly rules the mind.
—Spanish proverb

You may have been told at some point or another that your body is a temple —a saying we've always found somewhat confusing. But if you put it into the context of winter hiking and camping—when you're subjecting your body to an intense experience in a challenging environment—it's easy to see the importance of treating your body with the utmost respect. Your body is your most important tool in the backcountry, so you must do everything you can to keep it in top working condition. Drinking plenty of water and eating a generous, balanced diet will provide the foundation for your health.

Hydration

Our bodies are about 60 to 70 percent water and the parts we rely on most for winter travel—our muscles, lungs, and brain—contain an even higher percentage of water, functioning properly only when hydrated. Water is so important because it carries nutrients to our organs, transports oxygen to our cells, removes waste, and protects joints. Perhaps most noticeable in winter, water also transfers warmth from our heat-generating muscles to our cold-sensitive fingers and toes. Maintaining hydration is the best way to prevent hypothermia, lethargy, depression, and general fatigue.

We've all heard about the importance of drinking water to promote good health, but did you know drinking up during the winter when the air is dry is especially important? That puff of breath you see in front of your face is actually water vapor—lost moisture. When you inhale cold air, your nose, mouth, throat, and lungs warm it up, meaning the moist lining of your lungs loses fluid as they heat the incoming air. Breathing is another way you lose water, but perspiration, urination, and defecation also play a role.

Staying hydrated is easy to do—just drink often! Unfortunately, you can't rely on your body to signal when it's time for a drink, and by the time you feel thirsty, you're usually already dehydrated. The best way to keep tabs on your hydration is to occasionally check your urine. If it's clear and copious, you're in good shape. If your urine is dark, you are dehydrated, so drink up!

The general rule of thumb is that you should drink between 4 and 6 quarts per day, depending on the temperature, the amount of energy you're exerting, the altitude, sun exposure, and your body size (large adults need more water than small children). Do not chug all those quarts at once, though, as the human body can absorb only one liter of water each hour. Instead, drink approximately 100 milliliters every 15 to 30 minutes. Most of your intake should be cold water, but you can supplement it with flavored water, hot drinks, and soup to keep things interesting. You'll develop your own hydration habits over time. Until then, get in the habit of drinking a quart of water first thing in the morning, keeping water close by throughout the day—drinking some during every break—and having another quart before you crawl into your sleeping bag.

Water Sources and Treatment

Long gone are the days when you could plunge your bottle into a stream, fill it with cold, pristine mountain water, and start drinking. First of all, running water is challenging to find in winter. Secondly, even the purest-looking water can house microscopic parasites that are damaging to human health. Not even extreme cold will kill the waterborne parasites *Giardia lamblia* and *Cryptosporidium* that can wreak havoc on our gastrointestinal systems. By drinking untreated water, you risk ingesting these microscopic organisms and suffering the consequences—diarrhea, cramps, fatigue, and loss of appetite. Thankfully, simply treating water through boiling, filtration, or halogenation will make drinking safe. But keep reading, as not every method has the same effectiveness in winter.

Collecting Water

Locating water in liquid form is the first task. Some streams run even during the depths of winter, and liquid is always hiding somewhere beneath a lake's layers of snow and ice. However, taking water from natural sources can be quite hazardous; you must exercise great caution to avoid slipping, sliding, and falling into frozen lakes and rivers. Carefully check the thickness of ice before venturing out onto a frozen lake, and always have someone to spot you.

Once you've identified a good place to create a hole in the ice, start digging. Use something sharp—an ice ax works fine, but a chisel is more efficient—and maintain a safe distance from the thin edge of ice as you dig. Once the hole is complete, use a ski pole to help you access the water from a generous distance. Tie a string to the lid of your water bottle, loop the string around the end of the pole, and carefully lower the bottle into the hole to fill it up. Once you've

Sometimes you can find running streams from which to collect water. Be aware that accessing such streams does present hazards—snowy banks often overhang water, and the water must be treated.

Carefully retrieve water from beneath the snow and ice by lowering a bottle into a hole from a secure distance.

Keeping Your Water Liquefied

Even when the temperature plunges, you can prevent frozen water bottles. During the day, travel with your bottle enclosed in an insulating pouch or wrap extra clothing around it and keep it in the top of your pack. You can also wrap a thin cord around the water bottle's lid and wear the bottle around your neck, tucked beneath your outer later, so that it's accessible and protected. Once you reach camp, store extra bottles inside your tent or, if the temperature is extremely low, inside your sleeping bag. If you've melted snow for water, filled all your bottles, and still have some left over, bury the water-filled pot under a foot of snow—the water won't freeze overnight if it's buried under the snow. Just be sure to mark the spot so you can find it again, even if it snows a foot or two in the night. If your bottle does freeze, place it upside down in a pot of boiling water until you can remove the lid. Then pour a small amount of hot water into the bottle until some of the ice melts. Pour the remaining water and bits of ice into the pot to reheat, and keep repeating the process until all the ice has turned to liquid.

created the hole, make sure you mark it so you can access it later and no one will accidentally step into it.

Purifying Water

After collecting water, you can purify it either by boiling it or treating it with chemicals such as chlorine or iodine (see below). Filtering is not a viable option in winter because freezing temperatures tend to crack filters, making them useless (except as weights). Boiling is a tried and true method, though it does require time, a stove, a pot, and fuel. When boiling, don't bother achieving a rolling boil; just be sure you see at least one bubble before you turn off the stove.

Purifying with Iodine and Chlorine

Halogens, including iodine and chlorine, are disinfectants that kill pathogens in water. They are popular with winter hikers because they don't require stove setup or fuel. You will need merely to carry a little bottle of liquid chlorine or iodine (which also comes in tablet and crystal forms), add some to untreated water, and wait several minutes before drinking. When using chlorine,

From Snow to Water

Melting snow for drinking water requires snow, ample fuel, a pot, a lid, and some patience. An advantage to melting snow instead of finding water already in liquid form is that you don't have to treat the resulting water—as long as you have clean snow to start with. Be sure to use only pristine-looking snow (no yellow snow, indicating urine, or pink snow, indicating bacteria), and check occasionally as you dig through layers to be sure you don't notice something you wouldn't want to drink.

Put a little water in the pot before adding snow to melt. If absolutely no water is available, start with a tiny bit of snow and stir it constantly while it's melting. Then slowly add more and more snow into the pot until it's full. You'll be surprised by how little water comes from a full pot of snow—especially if you're using dry snow—but try not to become disheartened. Just continue adding snow slowly until your have the amount of water you desire. One way to speed up the process is to double-melt snow by placing a second pot full of snow on the lid of the first pot already melting. Any way you do it, monitor the melting process continually, as the particles in snow can easily scorch and leave your water with a very unpleasant flavor.

simply mix a few drops of chlorine with a few drops of water in the lid of your bottle, wait several minutes, and then pour the mixture into your water bottle and—voila!—it's treated. Iodine is as simple to use and is our preferred water treatment method. We drop two iodine tablets in each water bottle, wait 15 minutes, then slightly loosen the cap and shake the bottle to flush out untreated water through the bottle cap threads. Then we drink! If you find the flavor of iodine distasteful, add some sports drink powder or a neutralizer tablet. People have employed iodine as a water purifier only in recent history, so some question its impact on long-term human health. If you are uncomfortable with the unknown, stick with boiling—humans have done it since the first days of fire and our species still thrives.

Food

One of the many joys of winter hiking is that you can eat and eat—and eat some more—and you probably won't gain a pound. In actuality, the risk of losing weight and depleting your body's nutrients during a winter hiking trip is greater, which is just one reason why you should bring plenty of well-balanced foods into the backcountry. Tempt yourself with a variety of yummy, fatty foods. Fresh foods will take much longer to spoil in the cold than in the heat, so you can incorporate them into your meals and keep your menu enticing. By eating plenty of nutritious goodness, you'll maintain high energy and keep your mind sharp and your body responsive.

Pre-Trip Preparation

Plan your menu and prepare foods before leaving home. As discussed in Chapter 1, you should repackage food in plastic bags to eliminate the waste of cardboard packaging and to protect food against damage. Break solid foods, such as chocolate bars, into chunks, and pre-slice salami and other meats before hitting the trail. Label foods, such as powdered milk, parmesan, and lemonade mix, that look similar. Before purchasing food for the backcountry, think about its likelihood of freezing (cream cheese, for example, freezes quickly and becomes a useless block), its nutrients, its weight, and its preparation time. In general, you'll want quick, simple one-pot meals for breakfast and dinner, many snacks throughout the day, hearty trail lunches that don't require setting up a stove or boiling water, and plenty of fixings for hot drinks. When you're traveling and the cold is extreme, keep foods—especially snacks—close to your body and within reach. Bury foods in your pack that you won't immediately need and wrap them in insulating layers of clothing so they won't freeze.

A Balanced Diet

While water is the most important element of good nutrition, nourishment comes from a variety of food sources—carbohydrates, fats, and proteins. Carbohydrates are either simple or complex. Simple carbohydrates, such as sugar, honey, maple syrup, and candy, enter the blood stream almost immediately after ingestion and break down soon thereafter. When eating them, you'll receive an instant energy boost that won't last long but serves its purpose for a quick boost. To sustain that boost, look to complex carbohydrates (strings of simple sugars) such as pasta and grains. These foods provide fuel over many hours and are great for breakfasts and dinners when you need fuel to get you through the day or night. Approximately half of your menu should be composed of carbohydrates. Another 30 percent should come from fats from food such as cheeses, butter, meats, and nuts. Because fats break down very slowly, fatty foods are great energy sources to ingest before bed to keep you warm throughout the night. We often keep a hunk of chocolate near our pillows to nibble on in the middle of the night if we wake up cold. The final 20 percent of your foods should be comprised of proteins, which are prevalent in meat, dairy, nuts, beans and whole grains.

Enjoying Your Food

While planning a balanced diet that incorporates carbohydrates, fats, and proteins is important, bringing the foods you like to eat and eating a lot is essential. The food you bring will likely provide all the vitamins you need. But it won't hurt to bring some water-soluble B and C vitamins to share with the group. With growing kids, especially, we pass around a small bottle of chewable vitamin Cs after breakfast. If nothing else, the little tablets make kids *think* they're all powerful, full of energy, and immune to illness.

Meals are a little different in the winter woods than they are elsewhere or during other seasons. Mornings are a time of constant movement, so you'll want a simple, complete meal that provides the foundation for the day's energy needs. Standing around camp in the cold, early hours is useless and miserable, so boil some water and consider meals that can be prepared in people's thermal mugs after they enjoy a morning hot drink. Spice up instant oatmeal with dried fruits, cinnamon, and brown sugar. Salt your grits. Fry your bagels. Serve granola with hot milk and butter. When you have time, warmth, and ambition, make potato pancakes with potato pearls, pancake mix, and butter. Spread peanut butter over fried bagels. As long as the food is enticing, people will eat—and that, along with drinking plenty of water, is the key to starting the day on the right foot.

Breakfast Oatmeal, bagels, cream of rice or wheat, grits, granola, dried fruit, pancake mix, potato pearls (for potato pancakes and hash brown potatoes)

Lunch Tortillas, peanut butter, jelly, tuna, salami, pepperoni (sliced), cheese (sliced), jerky (beef, chicken, or soy), nuts, sesame sticks, energy bars, candy, trail mix, cookies

Dinner Pasta, rice, couscous, instant soup mix, bacon, sausage, macaroni and cheese, chili, burritos

Spices, condiments, etc. Salsa, sugar (and brown sugar), olive oil, salt, pepper, cayenne, garlic, cinnamon, tea, coffee, hot chocolate, butter, powdered milk, powdered juice

A common saying suggests that lunch begins after breakfast and continues through to dinner. Because you will be constantly burning calories, it makes sense that you will constantly replace them by snacking throughout the day. All group members should carry their own snack stash, complete with a few granola bars and a personalized bag of gorp (good old raisins and peanuts), supplemented with an endless array of goodies, including M&Ms, dried fruits, almonds, and sesame sticks. At least one group member should also carry lunch foods—meats, cheeses, breads, and cookies—that can be shared with everyone during breaks.

Dinner can be as simple or elaborate as you like. Boil water as soon as you reach camp so that everyone can enjoy a hot drink or instant soup while dinner is being prepared. Your meal should consist of a starch base (rice, noodles or pasta), with protein (cheese, sausage, tuna, or beans and fat—butter and oil). We find that macaroni and cheese is a familiar, hearty, and quick dinner that everyone enjoys. Other favorites include burritos (rice and beans in a tortilla) and fried pasta—yum! For an even simpler option, choose between the many tasty, easy-to-prep freeze-dried foods currently on the market. They're more expensive than other foods, but also lighter and more sophisticated (i.e., chicken teriyaki and lasagna with meat sauce). Plus, the ability to just add hot water is quite tempting—especially on those unforeseen long nights when you're thinking about foregoing dinner altogether and hitting the sack, because you're that exhausted. On extended trips, we supplement our rations with a few freeze-dried meals for just those nights. If you follow our lead, beware of the suggested serving sizes on freeze-dried foods: if the package says that the meal serves four, plan instead on it serving two—you're a winter explorer, not a summer hiker.

How Much to Eat and Drink

The thought of traveling outdoors in the winter can arouse anxiety in some people, particularly teens, and a young woman named Katie we traveled with a few years ago was no exception. She tried to mask her nervousness with the can-do attitude she was known for in her school, where she was a straight-A student, and among her friends, who all looked up to her as if she were a goddess. Katie was a perfectionist about everything from her math scores to her thin physique. On the day we packed for our week-long winter camping trip, laying out bag after bag of cubed cheeses and meats, sticks and sticks of butter, and heaps of chocolate, Katie thought, "There's no way I'm going to eat all those rich, fatty foods!" Of course, we didn't find out she was thinking this until days later when we probed into what was causing her deep lethargy and severe chill: She'd barely been eating. By her account, she'd eaten more during those past few days than she would ever have dreamt of eating in her "normal" day-to-day life, but that was still not nearly enough. Fortunately, she'd been drinking plenty of water, so she'd warded off the dangerous consequences of malnutrition, but she wouldn't improve without some food. As soon as we convinced her to join us for a big, hearty meal, she almost instantaneously felt warmer and more energized.

Plan to eat and drink about twice as much while winter hiking and camping as you would in your day-to-day life. The average American consumes 2,700 calories per day while leading a largely sedentary lifestyle, but the average winter hiker burns between 4,000 and 7,000 calories per day. On day trips, you will have the advantage of retreating to a warm house at the end of the day, enjoying a big dinner, and sleeping in your temperature-controlled bedroom. That said, you should always bring more food on day trips than you think you'll need. Experience will eventually teach you how much food to carry; until then, bring two extra energy bars per person (they weigh just a few ounces each), an additional bag of nuts or jerky, and one extra water bottle. The added weight will seem insignificant if you're forced to stay out longer than expected.

On a multiday trip, you will need even more calories and more water because you won't have the luxury of retreating to a temperature-controlled environment. Remember that your body is your furnace and you need to continually stoke it with food and water. A general rule is to bring 2.5 pounds of food per person per day on a moderate winter trip. This will provide each person with about 4,500 calories—enough to replenish the calories burned through exercise and basal metabolism. When planning a more strenuous trip or expecting extreme cold, pack additional food so each person will have 3 pounds of food each day.

For trips longer than a week, consider dropping a food cache at a designated point along your route. A cache will allow you to resupply during your journey so that you won't need to carry more than a week's worth of food at a time. Choose a point along your route that is easily accessible via a trailhead or road, and drop your cache there prior to setting out. Mark the point on your map. Because you won't rendezvous with your cache for many days, make sure to package food in double plastic bags to prevent moisture from leaking in, and mark the cache so that you can find it under a fresh foot of snow. Resupply day is always greatly anticipated, and it can be even more exciting if you include a few treats, such as clean socks and your favorite candy bars.

When in the field, you will become amazingly attuned to your body and its need for food. It's a strange and wonderful sensation to feel your body instantly warm up and become reenergized after a mouthful of chocolate. Rarely in our day-to-day lives are we reminded that food, in its most basic sense, is composed of calories—units of heat, a form of energy. Fuel your body with plenty of tasty, nutritious foods that you enjoy eating and you will likely stay happy, healthy, and warm.

Hygiene

When we were little kids and we'd start to feel ill, our parents would shoo us outside and tell us that fresh air would do us well. While we've come to learn that cold air and exercise aren't great once the flu already has its grip, we're both generally healthy and we credit that, in large part, to our exposure to the elements. Rarely does anyone get a cold while they're outside moving their blood and breathing fresh air in and out of their lungs. Unfortunately the same can't be said for gastrointestinal problems, which often strike when groups are sharing meals and working in communal kitchens. Stomach complaints, which are the most common medical problem people face in the backcountry, almost always result from poor hygiene. Fortunately, gastrointestinal issues can be avoided easily.

Hand washing is the single most effective way to stop the spread of germs. Use water and a touch of antibacterial soap, or use hand sanitizer with alcohol (though be sure to thoroughly dry your hands afterward, as wet skin in contact with alcohol tends to quickly become frostbitten). With young people who are still developing their hygiene habits—or actively ignoring them—we ritualize the following procedure during the first hour or two of our adventure: When one person returns to the group after taking a poop, he asks someone else to pour a few drops of hand sanitizer from the bottle onto his hands. In this way, we avoid the bottle of hand sanitizer becoming the source of contamination. This ritual also helps us, as group leaders, keep track of how often people are going to the bathroom—an important indicator of health.

Healthy habits should extend beyond the toilet. Mealtime is a common time for germs to spread, so everyone in the group should wash their hands prior to preparing meals, even if they haven't gone to the bathroom in a while. During the meal, people should avoid sharing water bottles, cups, and personal utensils. No one should eat off the group's serving spoon or sip from the group ladle. When snacks are passed around, everybody should pour group food from the bag into their hands and not reach into the bag. These practices may initially seem persnickety, but remember that you're creating healthy habits and setting a good example for excellent expedition behavior—the key to any adventure.

CHAPTER TEN
Winter's Hazards

Many people today see the wilderness as scary and unapproachable. Some wonder why we choose to leave the comforts of home and venture outside in the first place. Others see the allure, but worry that backcountry travel is too dangerous, especially during the winter. Friends often ask us why we risk our safety for a few days' adventure in the great snowy outdoors. After we spark their interest with tales of moonlight on white snow and fresh powder tracks on a clear blue day, we launch into a comparison between the dangers of day-to-day front country and backcountry life.

In the front country, we put ourselves into dangerous situations every time we strap ourselves into an automobile and hurtle down the highway at 70 miles per hour. Even when we obey all traffic laws and practice safe driving, other drivers who might not be so careful surround us. Now that's scary.

In the backcountry in winter, there are also significant hazards—wicked storms and potential icefall and avalanches, to name a few—but they can usually be anticipated and avoided. By no means can we control the environment, but we can control how we choose to explore it and the level of risk we're willing to take.

Whether in the heart of the city or the depths of the wilderness, we believe a little fear is healthy—it keeps us sharp and alive. It reminds us not to become complacent. Every place in the world has its hazards and the wilderness is no exception.

The best way to avoid winter hazards is to practice precaution, safety, and sound judgment throughout your journeys. Because not all injuries and illnesses can be avoided, however, we strongly advise that at least one member of your group gain advanced wilderness instruction and become certified as a wilderness first responder, especially if you plan to adventure more than an hour's distance away from trailheads.

Hypothermia

The biggest, most common, and most easily avoidable danger you face while winter hiking and camping is getting wet and cold. If you get too cold, you can quickly develop a hypothermic condition in which the core body temperature drops to a dangerous level. Left untreated, it can cause death. Fortunately, plenty of warning signs can help to identify the early stages of hypothermia in yourself and your companions.

Hypothermia is a progressive condition that presents a range of symptoms as your body temperature drops lower and lower over time. Initially, you might notice that it's more difficult to unwrap a granola bar or buckle a clasp than it was a half hour earlier. Loss of motor skills, accompanied by shivering, is a classic sign of mild hypothermia. A common response to mild hypothermia is a desire to go lie down and get warm, which lots of people attempt to do. As discussed throughout this book, however, it's difficult to get warm simply by slipping into a sleeping bag—you first need to generate heat for your insulating bag to trap. If you notice someone in your group heading to bed at an unusual hour, be sure to assess whether or not they are experiencing mild hypothermia.

From mild to extreme, sufferers of hypothermia progress through a series of symptoms known as the "umbles." After experiencing the previously noted loss of motor skills (the stumbles and fumbles), victims get the mumbles and grumbles. They lose their ability to clearly articulate their thoughts, yet they're obviously trying to convey a negative attitude about their experience or about life in general. If their body temperature continues to drop, they will violently shiver for a period, then stop shivering altogether and become cool to the touch. Their body will eventually turn a bluish color and their pulse will become weak and slow. The severely hypothermic person will die if left untreated.

The treatment for hypothermia depends on the stage the victim is in when treatment begins. The goal—and the biggest challenge—is recognizing early onset hypothermia and treating it before it progresses into a more dangerous condition. Treat mild to moderate hypothermia by moving the victim to a warm and dry environment, such as a tent, as quickly as possible. Get the victim changed into dry clothes and then help him or her get into a sleeping bag. The warmth generated by shivering will eventually warm him up, though he'll re-warm more quickly and be more comfortable if he has a few warm companions on either side of him, warm water bottles in his armpits and at his feet, some sips of a warm drink, and a few bites of food. If three people are in the group (including the victim), one person should zip a sleeping bag to the victim's bag and crawl in next to the victim while the third person heats water. If there are only two people (including the victim), it's more important that the victim have a warm body next to him than a warm water bottle in his armpit. He can also generate his own heat by doing a few sit-ups in his sleeping bag, though it's most imperative that he stay hydrated and take the time to rest and get warm.

More severely afflicted hypothermia victims should be treated with great care, preferably by someone who's received basic wilderness first-aid training. Severe hypothermia is an extreme medical emergency and its victims could suffer heart failure if handled roughly. Avoid the temptation to rub the victim's skin or move their joints, and do not encourage the victim to exercise or eat. The focus of treatment for severely hypothermic victims is the prevention of additional heat loss. After gently getting the victim inside a sleeping bag and on top of an insulating pad, surround him with additional insulation—extra sweaters and fleece jackets, hats, and even additional sleeping bags—and wrap the whole bundle in a windproof and waterproof layer, such as a tarp, tent fly, or reflective blanket. The resulting cocoon—also known as a hypothermia wrap—should leave only the patient's face exposed. While he continues to rest,

Medical Evacuations

Victims of severe hypothermia, full-thickness frostbite, fractures, and other injuries suffered in the field require timely medical attention. Before putting an evacuation plan into motion, pause and consider the urgency of the medical problem, the distance to the trailhead, the terrain, the weather, the mental and physical ability of the group, and all the various evacuation possibilities. Decide whether the whole group can walk or ski out and if the patient is capable of doing so without becoming more injured or ill. If not, two group members may have to go for help while others remain at camp. Self-evacuation is generally preferable when possible, as it's more straightforward and efficient. However, if the injury is severe (such as a neck injury), the terrain is challenging, and/or the group size is small, it may be best to send two group members for help while others stay and tend to the patient. The rescue party members should be strong, levelheaded, and adequately equipped for the journey with proper gear and plenty of food and water. They should also carry specific information about the status of the patient and the exact location of the group.

the other group members should prepare for an evacuation (see sidebar on page 161), as the victim will need professional medical attention quickly in order to return to a normal core body temperature.

Frostbite

On a recent snowshoe trip through Maine's Grafton Notch, the four people in our group eagerly anticipated the views from the top of Baldpate Mountain's West Peak. The saddle between the Baldpate's two peaks is notoriously wind-swept and exposed, and the conditions on that early March afternoon were no exception. The wind howled along the stretch of trail as we ventured toward the summit. We were feeling good and strong, generating heat through intense aerobic activity even though the temperature hovered around minus-30 with the wind chill.

To avoid overheating and sweating as we hiked upslope, we each removed our balaclavas, leaving our cheeks, chins, and noses exposed to the elements. We recognized that by exposing bare flesh to the extreme cold and wind, we were putting our skin at risk of freezing (becoming frostbitten). For that reason, we constantly monitored each other, looking to see if our skin was turning dark red or white and waxy. We took frequent, short breaks to check in with each other and drink some water. At one point, someone noticed that Lucas's nose was turning from pink to red, so he put on his balaclava and covered his nose. Because we all stayed well hydrated and practiced active layering throughout our journey, we were all able to reach the summit without experiencing any frostbite.

Frostbite, like hypothermia, is a progressive condition with effects ranging from no damage to substantial tissue loss at the site of freezing. Also like hypothermia, frostbite is completely preventable if winter hikers maintain awareness and exercise proper precautions. By insulating the body against the mechanisms of heat loss, you can avoid frostbite. This means that you should have all your skin covered when the cold is deep and the wind is howling. Frostbite usually occurs at the extremities of the body—toes, fingers, ears, and nose—so take extra precautions to shelter these parts from the elements, even if it means wearing a face mask and goggles, gloves and mittens, and a balaclava under a hood.

Frostbitten tissue in the early stages may be white, waxy, numb, and cold, but it will also be soft and pliable to the touch. The affected area can usually be warmed by direct contact with another person's warm skin—such as by putting bare feet against a companion's belly or placing fingers beneath armpits.

For more severe cases, when the frostbitten tissue is hard to the touch, professional medical attention should be sought immediately. If medical help isn't available, you can consider warming the tissue via an immersion bath (immersing the frostbitten part in water warmed to approximately 105 degrees), but note that this is not advisable if refreezing could occur. If a frostbitten area freezes after being thawed it will cause even greater damage to the tissue. Instead of warming, insulating the frozen tissue to prevent any further freezing and evacuating the victim is usually the best option.

Snow and Ice Hazards

Ice, storms, and avalanches are the especially dangerous hazards that come along with winter adventuring. While ice has its advantages—frozen lakes can provide smooth, even expressways for travel—and storms present an exhilarating beauty, avalanches offer no benefit to winter travelers. They're downright terrifying. But avalanches, like fallen ice and winter storms, are somewhat predictable. You can usually avoid everything from fallen ice to spruce traps and from tree wells to avalanches if you learn what they are, where they're likely to wreck havoc, and how to stay far, far away from them. Fortunately for those on the East Coast, avalanches aren't as common as they are on the West Coast. But in the east, winter storms are a real concern, as are the associated hazards of frostbite and hypothermia. Following are the most common winter hazards on the trail and basic information about how to avoid becoming a victim.

Falling Ice

Ice can fall from cliffs in large chunks and blocks or it can fall from trees in thin icicles. Whether bus-like or dagger-like, falling ice can be very dangerous, and victims have suffered everything from head injuries and nasty bruises to deep

Beware traveling beneath ice formations such as these, which could break off and cause serious damage to anything below.

If you do need to travel beneath ice-laden trees or cliffs, wear a helmet.

lacerations and crushed bones. To avoid falling ice, be especially aware when traveling below cliffs. Don't linger around those areas during—or immediately after—an ice storm, or when direct sunlight is hitting ice formations overhead. If you do have to make a crossing beneath ice-laden trees or cliffs during a potentially dangerous period, wear a helmet.

Spruce Traps

Small coniferous trees, such as a spruces and hemlocks, are more dangerous than you might imagine, especially when they're completely covered by a thin layer of snow that you're attempting to ski over or walk across with snowshoes. Because the little trees have so much dead air between their branches, and because their thin branches are weak, the trees can't hold a person's weight. You'll be happily skiing or tromping along your way when suddenly—whoomp!—you're waist-deep in snow. You've hit a spruce trap. Fortunately, trees don't grow on well-worn trails, so you can avoid these traps by simply sticking to the trail. When the trail is difficult to follow and you have to venture off it, spread your group out far enough so that you won't pile on top of each other should the leader plunge into a trap. However, everyone should be close enough so that someone can help if one person goes down.

Tree Wells

Tree wells are the rings of depressed snow around the bases of trees. These rings result when solar warmth radiates from the tree, so you'll find more tree wells in open forests where the sun reaches the ground. Should you come too close to the base of a tree and fall into its well, you may not be able to extract yourself without assistance. Fortunately, tree wells are easy to avoid—just keep a safe distance from them by maintaining control and moderating your speed while skiing. When you have to go to the bathroom and want to do so next to a tree, keep tree wells in mind—you'd hate to need a helping hand when you're in a compromising position!

Undercut Snow

With undercut snow, a thick blanket of snow appears to cover the ground, but that layer is actually quite thin and unstable. This happens because sometimes snow beneath the surface melts more quickly than surface snow, particularly where water is present. Stay away from the lowest valley points, where silent streams may undercut the snow. By probing ahead with your ski or trekking pole, you can avoid plunging through thin snow and into icy water.

Avoid the depressions, called tree wells, that form around the bases of trees.

Traveling through heavy wind can be very challenging, as this hiker can attest to.

Hidden Obstacles

Even the most mammoth rocks and logs can hide beneath the surface when snow levels are high. This especially presents a hazard to skiers, who tend to build momentum and speed as they glide along. Skiers can avoid having their skis slide beneath a buried log or slamming into a covered boulder if they stick to packed trails.

Winter Storms

Winter storms can escalate quickly and become inhospitable to winter travelers. Refer to Chapter 6 for more information about assessing winter weather, anticipating storms, and staying out of their path. If you do find yourself trapped in a winter storm, seek shelter from the wind. Look for a sheltered area on the leeward side of large boulders or in the middle of a large stand of mature trees. If taking shelter in a wooded area, look to the tops of the trees to make sure none are dead and at risk of falling. If you have the time and energy to put up a tent or build a snow shelter or snow trench, do so. Wait out the storm while staying warm, dry, and hydrated.

Whiteouts

Winter storms and whiteouts tend to go hand-in-hand, as high winds dominate both. When the wind whips falling snow and the snow from the ground into a featureless froth of milky white, visibility is reduced to nothing. Whiteouts can be very disorienting and dangerous, but they rarely "come out of nowhere." When the wind picks up and you're in an open area full of dry snow, expect that a whiteout is brewing. Note the major landmarks surrounding you while you can still see them. That way, if you can't afford to hunker down and wait out the squall, you can still take and follow a compass bearing toward your intended destination.

Avalanches

Simply stated, an avalanche is any large amount of snow sliding down a slope. This may sound straightforward, but avalanches are actually quite complex and challenging to predict and avoid. Many people have spent their whole lives studying avalanches, and wonderful books have been published that focus solely on analyzing snow stability and avalanche hazard. Similarly, multiday avalanche seminars are offered throughout the nation, and we highly advise anyone traveling in the backcountry during winter to take such a course. Check with your local outdoor gear retailers, hiking clubs, and search-and-rescue groups to learn about what is offered in your area. The following merely provides the basic information you need to know, but it is not intended to substitute for an avalanche seminar taught in the field by professionally trained and certified guides. Even if you plan to travel far from avalanche terrain, you—and every other winter traveler—should build a fundamental understanding of where avalanches occur and how to avoid them.

Avalanches come in many types, from masses of loosely packed snow sliding down slope at a leisurely pace to colossal slabs of snow accelerating downhill at more than 100 miles an hour. The speed of an avalanche depends on the slope and size of the mountain, as well as the friction the snow encounters as it moves downhill. As sliding snow builds momentum, it picks up trees, rocks, skiers, and snowshoers—anything that can be lifted up in the "wave" of snow. People caught in avalanches usually end up buried deep beneath the snow, a scary and potentially deadly outcome that should be avoided at all costs. Most avalanche victims are unable to identify unstable snow conditions or high-risk terrain. Other victims have learned about avalanches, but become complacent after years of avalanche-free escapades in the backcountry. Whether you're a novice or an expert, you must always maintain awareness about avalanche conditions.

An avalanche is highly likely to occur on a mountain with a slope of 30 to 45 degrees if a triggering mechanism hits the slope when it has substantial snow and at least one weak layer. A triggering mechanism comes in the form

Know Your Avalanche Basics

- The most dangerous time to travel in an avalanche-prone area is during or within the first 24 hours after heavy snowfall, high winds and rain, or a quick thaw.
- Avalanche terrain lies on a slope, and the majority of slopes that avalanche are treeless and between 30 and 45 degrees.
- Take an avalanche seminar to learn how to assess snowpack conditions and respond appropriately, should an avalanche occur.
- When traveling in avalanche country, always wear an avalanche beacon and know how to use it. An avalanche beacon is a small, single-frequency radio that transmits a steady beep when in *send* mode. When switched to *receive* mode, it picks up beeps from transmitting beacons. The stronger the signal, the closer the *sending* and *receiving* beacons are, and therefore the closer the rescuer is to the victim.

of additional weight—either a fresh layer of quickly accumulated snow or a passing skier or hiker who crosses the release zone (the area near or at the top of the avalanche path, where unstable snow breaks loose). Weight triggers one of two types of avalanches, either a loose snow, or point-of-release, avalanche or a slab avalanche, which starts when a large amount of snow fractures off the slope in an obvious line. Slab avalanches are more dangerous, so we'll focus primarily on how to avoid them.

The first step to avoiding a slab avalanche is recognizing where they are and are not likely to occur. Good pre-trip planning is fundamental. Before heading into a wilderness area, inquire with the nearest governmental land agency about avalanche dangers in that region. Some agencies and ski areas publish daily avalanche reports on the Internet, but keep in mind that terrain and snow conditions vary greatly, even within a small area. Inquire about recommended routes that are generally safe from avalanche dangers, and stay on winter-use trails, which rarely cross dangerous terrain. If you're unsure about avalanche conditions and want to travel into an area with the confidence that an avalanche won't occur (as we often do when we're traveling with beginners or leading a group of children), stay on flat or gently rolling terrain. Heavily forested areas are usually protected from avalanches, too.

If you do decide to venture into an area where some risk of avalanches exists, it's important that you are able to determine whether or not the snow is stable and identify which slopes present the most danger. During avalanche seminars, instructors will teach you how to dig a test pit to expose a cross-section of the snowpack and determine whether any of the layers exhibit weaknesses. At least one person in your group should have gone through a seminar prior to your trip and be able to teach other group members how to safely dig and read a snow pit. Another method, albeit less accurate, is to probe the snowpack with a pole. If the pole confronts an uneven layer as it descends (the layer will feel more coarse and grainy), then the snowpack is unstable; if the snowpack feels cohesive and firm, however, the layers are well bonded.

Once you've determined whether or not the snowpack is stable, examine the terrain. Often the most inviting slopes—open bowls powdered with fresh, deep snow or perfect black diamond-like runs, for example—are most prone to slide. Before traversing any slope, look up and identify how much snow is above you. Look around to see whether evidence of a past avalanche exists—often an avalanche-prone area will slide more than once. (Telltale signs of past avalanches include flattened trees and branches, steep ravines with no growth, and piles of dirty snow beneath slopes.) Check out the aspect of the slope, which is the direction to which the mountain slope faces. Narrow drainages and gullies with snow-laden sides should be avoided when the snowpack is unstable. Similarly, choose not to travel narrow ridges that have cornices (overhanging masses of snow or ice created by wind) that could easily break off and send you sliding. Lastly, listen for warning signs: even on level ground, an unstable snowpack will often settle with a haunting "whoomph" underfoot. Whenever you hear snowpack settle, notice signs of previous avalanches, or identify conditions conducive to sliding, take extra precaution.

Crossing an avalanche zone is a very risky endeavor that we do not recommend. However, we recognize that backcountry travel does involve taking some calculated risks. Should you decide to cross a slope after determining that the risk of an avalanche is low, you should still employ these precautions when traveling in avalanche country:

- Wear additional clothing and make sure your outer shell is zipped completely and closed at the cuffs. Should you become trapped beneath the snow, the extra clothing will help trap warmth close to your body and the outer layers will prevent snow from coming in contact with your skin.
- Unclip your pack's chest and waist buckles, loosen your snowshoe or ski bindings, and free your wrists from pole straps. By detaching yourself from your gear, you will be able to shed it more easily in case of an emergency.
- Have everyone in the group switch their avalanche beacons to the transmitting mode and secure them inside their clothing. Avalanche beacons transmit a signal that can be picked up by other beacons in the area when they are switched into the receiving mode. Using an avalanche beacon can greatly reduce the amount of time spent searching, probing, and digging for a victim during an avalanche rescue.

Only one person should traverse the slope at a time. Other group members should stand safely to the side in an area where they can see the entire slope and the person crossing. The person making the traverse should continue slowly and steadily until clear of the danger zone. Only after the first person has made it completely across should the second person start the traverse.

Should you find yourself caught in a slide, you must act quickly, yet try to remain calm and take these actions:

- Yell to alert your group mates that you're caught in a slide.
- Shrug off your pack and try to get to an area outside the slide as quickly as possible.

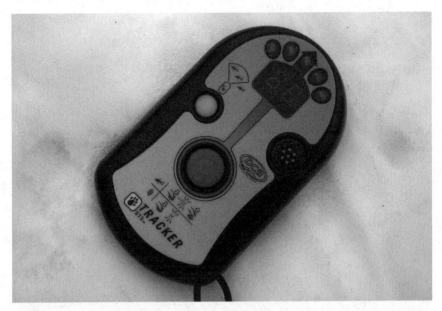

Avalanche beacons transmit signals that can be picked up by other beacons to aid in locating an avalanche victim.

- If you can't get to a safe place on the side of the slide, try to stay "above water" by making swimming motions.
- If your feet hit a hard surface, push aggressively against it to try to propel yourself up and out of the torrent's grasp.
- Immediately before the snow settles around you, attempt to surround yourself with air pockets. Punch out snow in front of your face to create breathing space. Shake your head and wriggle around. Take a deep breath to expand the breathing room around your torso. If possible, punch a hand up through the surface and try to dig yourself out.

Wait. You can survive an avalanche as long as you stay calm and your rescuers find you within 30 minutes. Your chances of survival greatly diminish after the first half hour.

If one of your companions gets caught in a slide, keep your eyes on the exact spot where that person was last seen. Don't remove your eyes from that spot until you mark it with a pole or ski. Then follow these steps:

1. Set your avalanche beacon to "receive" and hone in on the location of the victim.

Snow shovels are lightweight and easy to break down and store on the outside of your pack.

2. Stand shoulder-to-shoulder with other group members and probe continuously as you slowly advance in a line.
3. Probe deeply, as the victim could be buried under multiple feet of snow.
4. When the probe hits something soft and giving (unlike a rock, which will feel hard), start digging until you uncover the victim.

Once located, the victim should be handled carefully; traumatic head and neck injuries may have occurred. The victim should be treated for shock and hypothermia and examined for any other injuries, such as fractures, lacerations, or frostbite. If they are determined not to have a traumatic head or neck injury, move them out of avalanche danger and seek help.

Other Winter Hazards

Many other injuries and afflictions are possible in the backcountry, whether it's winter, spring, summer, or fall. Along with common ailments that affect wilderness travelers any time of year (sunburn, headaches, stomachaches, blisters, and sprains, to name a few), winter enthusiasts must take preventative measures against two additional afflictions—snow blindness and trench foot.

These South American explorers stop on the trail for some quick blister care. Always fix hot spots before they become bigger problems.

Snow Blindness

Snow blindness is sunburn of the eyes. It occurs in winter when your eyes are not properly protected from the harmful sun rays that reflect off the snow's surface. Though the victim doesn't become truly "blind" (recovery almost always occurs within two or three days of resting), significant pain, blurred vision, and red, swollen eyes will be present until treatment is administered. A patient experiencing snow blindness should be treated with cool, wet compresses applied gently to the eyelids. Have the patient rest for 24 to 48 hours until the symptoms subside. Snow blindness can be prevented by wearing sunglasses that block UV light; if traveling over snow fields or glaciers, glasses should also have side flaps that prevent peripheral light from entering.

Trench Foot

Also known as immersion foot, trench foot is a common cold-weather injury that was a particular problem for soldiers in trench warfare during the winters of World Wars I and II and the Vietnam War. When tissue is in prolonged contact with cold and moisture, circulation becomes poor and the tissue eventually becomes damaged. As with all other cold-weather afflictions, symptoms are exacerbated by poor hydration and malnutrition. To prevent trench foot, stay hydrated and make sure that your feet are warm and dry and experiencing good circulation throughout each night. As noted in Chapter 8, we each keep a dry pair of socks at the foot of our sleeping bag and change into them before bed every night. Even if you forget to dry your wet socks on your thighs during the night and you need to change back into them in the morning, you will avoid trench foot by returning to the dry socks the following night.

Headaches

Headaches might be the most common ailment in the world, and in the back-country it is no exception. We've all had them, and we've felt how a dull, mildly discomforting ache differs from a throbbing and debilitating pain. Most head-aches start slowly and can be stopped in their tracks with a little rest and hydration. In the wild outdoors, head pain is usually associated either with muscular tightness in the back of the neck (called tension headaches) or, more likely still, with dehydration. To avoid tension headaches, make sure you sleep on a comfortable sleeping pad at night; during the day, hike with a well-fitting pack. If you feel that the weight you are carrying is contributing to your neck tension, ask a companion to take some heavier items from your pack. To prevent dehydration headaches, drink regularly (see Chapter 9). To treat either a tension or dehydration headache, rest. Slowly drink at least a liter of water. If your pain does not quickly subside, take an over-the-counter painkiller. Headaches rarely indicate life-threatening illnesses, unless they are accompanied by other symptoms. However, if someone suddenly experiences a severe headache with a pain unlike anything felt before, and if that pain persists for 24 hours unre-lieved by rest, hydration, and painkillers, the person should be evacuated to a doctor as soon as possible.

Stomachaches

The most common abdominal illness in the backcountry is gastroenteritis, an inflammation of the gastrointestinal tract. It is generally caused by poor camp hygiene (see Chapter 9) and generally resolves itself in a day or two. Symptoms include discomfort throughout the abdominal area (often called stomachaches) with occasional cramping. Diarrhea is also a common symptom, and some people may complain of nausea. Most people with gastroenteritis have very low energy and experience great discomfort. Treat them by allowing them to rest and giving them water. Consider giving them anti-diarrheal medications, too, and monitor them for signs of serious illness, such as fever rising above 101 degrees or blood in the stools. If more serious symptoms begin, seek medical attention.

Strains and Sprains

Strains are injuries to muscle fibers or tendons, and sprains are injuries to ligaments. Both are considered athletic injuries, resulting when the fibers, tendons, or ligaments are stretched too far. If you experience a strain or sprain, you'll feel pain at the source and see considerable discoloration and some swelling. Treat the affected area with rest, ice, compression, and elevation (RICE). In other words, if you strain your ankle, follow these steps: stop using your ankle and let it rest; cool it with an ice pack (or snow pack), wrap it with an elastic bandage, and prop it up so that when you are lying or sitting, it is elevated above your heart. If the injury is severe and you cannot put any weight on your ankle, put a medical evacuation plan into motion (see sidebar on page 161). With proper care, your ankle will be back to normal within two to six weeks.

CHAPTER ELEVEN
After Your Journey

We shall not cease from exploration,
and the end of all our exploring
will be to arrive where we started
and know the place for the first time.
— T.S. Eliot, *Little Gidding*

Every time we return home after a winter hiking and camping trip, we go through a similar routine: we lay our gear out to dry, wash ourselves and our laundry, dress in soft, plush cotton, eat a huge dinner, drink lots of water, and collapse on the couch. Only then are we struck by what we've just accomplished: We comfortably traveled in the winter woods! We usually ruminate on this for a while, laughing about particular incidents, downloading photos from our digital camera, and calling friends and family to let them know we made it home safely and to share stories from our adventure. Throughout the routine, we're struck again and again by simple conveniences—a flushing toilet, a light switch, a thermostat, and even a telephone. Having just spent days going to the bathroom outdoors, living by the light cycles of the natural world, creating warmth through food and exercise, and often traveling in silence, we're reminded that the modern utilities of day-to-day life require energy, and we approach them more mindfully.

Our awareness of energy consumption isn't all that becomes heightened after returning home from the wintry woods—our awareness about most everything improves. After enjoying a quiet, pristine backcountry, the stimulants of urban living become pronounced. Though we thoroughly enjoy our home life—our friends, the cultural opportunities waiting around the corner—we always take solace knowing we can escape from the city and head for the woods whenever we get the urge. Unfortunately, wild lands are becoming more scarce as land is being developed for housing, resorts, and golf courses. Returning to the city after a winter hiking trip, we're reminded that not everyone values the wilderness as much as we do. We're reminded that we, the people who recreate in the wilderness and care deeply for the wildlife and ecosystems it supports, have an opportunity and an obligation to help protect public lands and encourage others to get outside and explore.

Giving Back to Public Lands

Many hikers have worked to maintain the public trails that they use. We're often reminded of this during the summer, when we pass volunteer work crews on the trail. But crews put away their shovels and hang up their hard hats once a thick blanket of snow covers the ground. As we travel through the backcountry in winter, it's easy to convince ourselves that the wilderness is pristine, that we're the only people in the world who use the trail, and that it will always be here for us. In fact, many public lands stay accessible year-round only through the help of a dedicated group of volunteers. Fall work parties prep for winter by clearing drainages, trimming brush, and rerouting trails to more durable surfaces. Trails need almost constant attention to stay open, and it's easy, fun, and rewarding for anyone to get involved in volunteer trail work.

Throughout the year, land agencies and non-governmental organizations offer volunteer opportunities on federal, state, and local public lands. Seasoned trail supervisors—experienced leaders who are familiar with the area—usually lead the work parties, supply the tools, and teach volunteers everything they need to know in order to contribute effectively to the project. Typical projects include cutting back brush, installing water bars, replacing rotten plank bridges, and closing unofficial trails for restoration purposes. The work is physical and rewarding, a good substitute for a few hours at the gym.

To find out about volunteer opportunities on the trails you frequent, contact the land management agency or outdoor recreation organization in your area. The Appalachian Mountain Club, for example, offers a wide range of volunteer opportunities with regional chapters. Another way to get involved is by participating in National Trails Day or National Public Lands Day. National Trails Day falls on the first Saturday of every June, when more than a million people around the country take part in events celebrating America's trails, including new trail dedications, workshops, educational exhibits, trail maintenance parties, and more. National Public Lands Day, hosted every September by the Bureau of Land Management and the Forest Service, is the nation's largest hands-on volunteer effort to improve and enhance public lands. Volunteers learn about critical natural resource issues while getting their hands dirty alongside other stewards of the land.

Trail work is the perfect combination of community service, outdoor awareness, physical exercise, and camaraderie. Volunteering outside with a group of like-minded people benefits the land, of course, but it can also be advantageous to the volunteer's development as a backcountry adventurer. Work party leaders and volunteers exchange tips about hiking routes, areas to see wildlife, trail hazards, and good camping sites in the area. Volunteers often develop life-long friendships on the trail and discover new hiking partners whose skill sets complement their own.

Volunteering on public lands will help you become invested in the area and its future. As a winter hiker, you'll experience a more fulfilling journey if you've done your part to maintain the trails you travel. Public lands belong to all of us, yet we are more likely to take care of them only after getting to know them from multiple perspectives—as a trail crew worker, a summer hiker, and a winter adventurer. By working on the trails, you'll probably become protective of them, particularly if they are threatened by development or land use. By protecting the trails, you help protect the land surrounding them.

Leading Others

One of the best ways to build your skills and experience and to give back to the land is by sharing your experiences and leading others in the outdoors. Some people—especially today's youth—are uncomfortable with spending more than hour away from their televisions, computers, and cell phones and have minimal experience recreating outdoors. Other people are comfortable exploring the outdoors in the warmer months, but find the idea of traveling in the cold daunting. Still others have the ambition to go winter hiking and camping but not the skills and experience to travel safely in the backcountry. When you feel comfortable hiking and camping in winter, and you're confident that you can take care of yourself, consider sharing your skills by giving presentations, leading friends and family, or even becoming a hiking guide. We truly believe that if people enjoy positive experiences in the outdoors, they are more likely to value the land, its resources, and the wild plants and animals it supports. You probably share our desire to preserve the wilderness for future generations, so please join us in spreading the word and getting more people involved in outdoor recreation and preservation.

Giving Presentations

A simple, straightforward, and effective thing that you can do to engage others is to talk openly and honestly about your winter hiking and camping adventures. We all have the tendency to embellish stories and exaggerate descriptions of the challenges we faced and overcame while braving the elements, but keep in mind your audience, and try to be accurate as you talk about your experience. If children hear that winter hiking and near-death experiences are synonymous, they will never want to go outside in the cold. If adults who already fear the wilderness hear that the wintry woods are chock full of dangers, their anxieties will become aggravated. Many people in the world believe that the wilderness should be tamed; please do not fuel their fire by inflating your stories of daring adventures. At the same time, be honest about the challenges that winter hiking and camping do present. People need to understand the importance of entering the wintry wilderness well prepared and well equipped.

Along with discussing your experiences with friends and family, talk to strangers and consider making public presentations. Many outdoor clubs, school programs, and church groups offer informal forums for such presentations. Show photographs and tell personal stories to help illustrate the point you are trying to make about a particular skill or lesson you learned on the trail. Always allow time for a question-and-answer period, and express genuine interest in people's comments and concerns. If you don't know the answer to a question, say so. You will build more trust from your audience if you're honest about what you do and do not know. If you can't respond to particular questions, assure people you will find the answers, and then get back to them with your reply in a timely manner.

Trips with Friends and Family

Share the adventure by encouraging your friends and family to join you on winter hiking trips. People may be reluctant to do so, fearing that you will push them beyond their comfort zone and ask them to hike farther and faster than they're physically capable of doing. The best way to overcome this obstacle is to suggest short, easy hikes and get them involved in the planning process. Ask questions about the aspects of winter travel that appeal to them, and then focus on incorporating those into your route. If you want to get your mom outside, and she's interested in photography, chose a scenic route that will present multiple photo opportunities. If she loves wildlife, carry along some field guides and take your time on the trail looking for tracks and other signs of life (see Chapter 1). If you want to take along your clumsy old friend, who usually stays away from sports that highlight his graceless lack of coordination, hang up the skis and have him use only snowshoes for the first few hikes.

Formal Leadership Opportunities

Plenty of people outside your circle of family and friends could benefit from your leadership on winter hiking and camping trips. Outdoor clubs, after-school programs, Boy Scout and Girl Scout troops, and environmental education organizations are always looking for knowledgeable, experienced leaders. While most outdoor guides are volunteers, paid positions exist for people with significant training and a demonstrated ability to lead successfully.

You should successfully complete at least ten multiday winter camping excursions before leading your first winter hiking and camping trip. Then make sure you're as ready as can be. Get yourself in shape, improving your physical strength and endurance. Refresh yourself on any knowledge of technical aspects that the trip will require. You don't necessarily have to be the most technically competent person in the group, however, as long as other group leaders possess the skills you lack. When we lead groups in the backcountry, for example, we rely on the fact that one of us has significant wilderness medicine training

A volunteer guide leads a group of teenagers on a trip around Mount Rainier, Washington.

and the other is a wizard with climbing ropes and mountaineering techniques. Along with everything else that goes into planning any trip (see Chapter 2), a trip leader has the added responsibility of assessing the qualifications of the people coming on the trip and communicating with them about trip details.

Guiding others into the woods in winter requires more than mere technical skills; it also requires strong leadership skills. Along with the skills you've learned during your winter outings and from this book—everything from trip planning, navigation, and nutrition to how to avoid hypothermia—you must be skilled at the "softer" elements of good leadership such as conflict resolution, compassion, and creative problem solving. You also must be comfortable in the role of leader.

Earning the trust of the group members and leading with patience is important. Winter hiking and camping can be challenging and beginners often feel their most vulnerable, sensitive selves come to the surface. Express genuine care for those you lead, and try to put yourself in their boots. Believe in them and they will be inspired to meet your vision, especially if you acknowledge their strengths and contributions. If they make mistakes, correct them carefully and in private, unless you feel the whole group could learn from the lesson. As you continue on the trail, stay positive and flexible—coach and give as often as you listen and receive. Strong leaders take group members' input into consideration before making decisions. However, understand that not every decision you make will be the popular one, and sometimes you can't stop to consult the group when safety is a concern. Leading is not always easy, but more often than not it's extremely rewarding.

Whether you're talking to your friends about a recent winter hiking trip, or you're leading a group of teenagers into the woods for the first time in their lives, you should feel good about the meaningful service you are providing your community. Every time you lead, you learn. Every time you share your experiences, they become more meaningful and engrained in your personal history.

Packing List: Day Trip

The following list describes the basic clothing and gear we each bring on a day hike when we are expecting the temperature to stay above zero:

Head-to-Toe Clothing

- ❏ Liner hat
- ❏ Fleece ski hat
- ❏ Baseball cap
- ❏ Sunglasses
- ❏ Goggles
- ❏ Lightweight long underwear top
- ❏ Midweight long underwear top
- ❏ Pile sweater
- ❏ Pile vest
- ❏ Waterproof/breathable shell jacket

- ❏ Liner gloves
- ❏ Insulating gloves or mittens
- ❏ Shell mittens
- ❏ Lightweight long underwear pants
- ❏ Waterproof/breathable pants or bibs
- ❏ Liner socks
- ❏ Wool socks (wear one and bring an extra pair)
- ❏ Gaiters
- ❏ Boots

Traveling Gear

- ❏ Snowshoes or cross-country skis
- ❏ Trekking poles or ski poles
- ❏ Day pack
- ❏ First-aid kit
- ❏ Map
- ❏ Compass

- ❏ Water bottles (2)
- ❏ Headlamp
- ❏ Pocket knife
- ❏ Waterproof matches
- ❏ Fire starter
- ❏ Snow shovel

Food

- ❏ Gorp (nuts, seeds, dried fruit, M&Ms)
- ❏ Jerky
- ❏ Energy bars (2)
- ❏ Bagels

- ❏ Cheese
- ❏ Salami
- ❏ Sesame sticks

Packing List: Camping Trip

If we're heading out on an overnight trip, we bring everything on the Day Trip Packing List and add the following:

Clothing

- ❏ Balaclava
- ❏ Parka with full hood
- ❏ Fleece pants with full side zippers
- ❏ Second fleece or wool sweater
- ❏ Second pair of liner socks
- ❏ Third pair of wool socks
- ❏ Camp booties

Individual Traveling and Camping Gear

- ❏ Large internal-frame backpack
- ❏ Snow shovel
- ❏ Sleeping bag
- ❏ Sleeping pads (one long and one short)
- ❏ Personal bowl
- ❏ Personal spoon (or spork)
- ❏ Personal insulated mug
- ❏ Toothbrush
- ❏ Toothpaste
- ❏ Personal items (e.g. corrective eyewear, feminine products, etc.)
- ❏ Ziploc bags (2 or 3)

Group Traveling and Camping Gear

- ❏ Tent
- ❏ Snow stakes
- ❏ Stove
- ❏ Stove platform
- ❏ Fuel
- ❏ Lighter
- ❏ Cooking pot
- ❏ Large spoon
- ❏ P-cord
- ❏ Garbage bag

Food and Water

- [ ] Water purification tablets (iodine)
- [ ] Powdered sports drink
- [ ] Hot chocolate
- [ ] Instant oatmeal
- [ ] Dried fruit
- [ ] Second bag of gorp
- [ ] Second bag of sesame sticks
- [ ] Third energy bar
- [ ] Additional bagels
- [ ] Additional cheese
- [ ] Fig Newtons
- [ ] Instant soup
- [ ] Freeze-dried dinner
- [ ] Spices
- [ ] Olive oil
- [ ] Chocolate

Optional Items

- [ ] Sled
- [ ] Snow saw
- [ ] Altimeter
- [ ] Barometer
- [ ] Insulated water bottle sleeve
- [ ] Hydration system (e.g., CamelBak)
- [ ] Field guide
- [ ] Playing cards
- [ ] Candle lantern
- [ ] Wisk brush (for sweeping snow from tent)
- [ ] Bandana
- [ ] Vapor-barrier socks
- [ ] Binoculars
- [ ] Camera
- [ ] Journal
- [ ] Small book
- [ ] Toilet paper
- [ ] Chemical heat pads

Extreme Conditions

For more extreme conditions, or when traveling in avalanche terrain, we also bring the following:

- [ ] Expedition-weight long underwear tops and bottoms
- [ ] Avalanche beacon
- [ ] Avalanche probe
- [ ] Skins for alpine skis
- [ ] Ice ax
- [ ] Crampons
- [ ] Extensive first-aid kit

APPENDIX C

First-Aid Kit

Prepare yourself for treating common backcountry ailments by assembling a first-aid kit with the following items:

- ❏ Adhesive strips (e.g. Band-Aids)
- ❏ Sterile gauze pads
- ❏ Athletic tape
- ❏ Wound closure strips (e.g. butterfly Band-Aids or Steri-Strips)
- ❏ Moleskin
- ❏ Large trauma dressings or individually wrapped sanitary napkins
- ❏ Alcohol wipes
- ❏ Lightweight splint (e.g. SAM Splint)
- ❏ Ace bandage
- ❏ Roll of gauze bandaging
- ❏ Ibuprofen
- ❏ Analgesic (e.g. aspirin)
- ❏ Antihistamine (e.g. Benadryl)

- ❏ Anti-diarrheal (e.g. Imodium)
- ❏ Anti-fungal (e.g. Tinactin)
- ❏ Decongestant (e.g. Sudafed)
- ❏ Antacid (e.g. Mylanta)
- ❏ Personal medications
- ❏ Hydrocortisone ointment
- ❏ Throat lozenges
- ❏ Rubber gloves
- ❏ Trauma shears
- ❏ Tweezers
- ❏ Irrigation syringe
- ❏ Sunscreen
- ❏ Lip balm
- ❏ Safety pins
- ❏ Tweezers

If you're heading out for a winter camping trip in a remote location or you're traveling for more than a week, consult your doctor before putting together your first-aid kit.

Resources

Developing Your Outdoor Skills

Reading books like this one is a great way to start your winter hiking and camping education. However, there is nothing quite like getting outside and giving it a try. The following outdoor instruction schools are based on experiential education—you learn by doing—and the instructors are highly trained. Here is a small sampling of the many outdoors organizations that offer winter hiking and camping courses. Contact the schools directly to learn about their offerings.

Adirondack Mountain Club
814 Goggins Road
Lake George, NY 12845
518-668-4447
www.adk.org

Appalachian Mountain Club
5 Joy Street
Boston, MA 02108
617-523-0655
www.outdoors.org
The AMC's New Hampshire Chapter offers workshops annually.

Green Mountain Club
4711 Waterbury-Stowe Road
Waterbury Center, VT 05677
802-244-7037
www.greenmountainclub.org

Mazamas
527 SE 43rd Avenue
Portland OR 97215
503-227-2345
www.mazamas.org

The Mountaineers
300 Third Avenue West
Seattle, WA 98119
206-284-6310
www.mountaineers.org

National Outdoor Leadership School (NOLS)
284 Lincoln Street
Lander, WY 82520
307-332-5300
www.nols.edu

Outward Bound
100 Mystery Point Road
Garrison, NY 10524
845-424-4000
www.outwardbound.org

U.S. Forest Service
National Avalanche Center
www.avalanche.org
Offers information about avalanche
safety seminars around the country.

Suggested Reading

Burns, Bob, and Mike Burns. *Wilderness Navigation: Finding Your Way Using Map, Compass, Altimeter, and GPS, 2nd Edition.* (Seattle: The Mountaineers Books, 2004).

Giesbrecht, Gordon, and James A. Wilkerson. *Hypothermia, Frostbite, and Other Cold Injuries: Prevention, Survival, Rescue, and Treatment, 2nd Edition.* (Seattle: The Mountaineers Books, 2006).

Goodman, David. *Backcountry Skiing Adventures: Classic Ski and Snowboard Tours in Maine and New Hampshire.* (Boston: AMC Books, 1998).

Goodman, David. *Backcountry Skiing Adventures: Classic Ski and Snowboard Tours in Vermont and New York.* (Boston: AMC Books, 2000).

Heid, Matt. *AMC's Best Backpacking in New England.* (Boston: AMC Books, 2008).

Kosseff, Alex. *AMC Guide to Outdoor Leadership.* (Boston: AMC Books, 2003).

Marchand, Peter. *North Woods.* (Boston: AMC Books, 1987).

McGivney, Annette. *Leave No Trace: A Guide to the New Wilderness Etiquette.* (Seattle: The Mountaineers Books, 2003).

Miller, Dorcas S. *Backcountry Cooking: From Pack to Plate in 10 Minutes.* (Seattle: The Mountaineers Books, 1998).

Tilton, Buck. *Outdoor Safety Handbook.* (Mechanicsburg, PA: Stackpole Books, 2006).

About the Authors

Lucas St. Clair and Yemaya Maurer are a husband-and-wife team with 20 years of combined experience teaching backcountry camping skills. They met on a semester mountaineering and kayaking program through the National Outdoor Leadership School (NOLS) in Patagonia, Chile, in 1998 and have since traveled the world together exploring wild lands. For years, Maurer managed the Student Conservation Association's Seattle-based program engaging urban youth in hands-on conservation and outdoor recreation. She currently works as a freelance writer covering outdoor recreation and local conservation issues. St. Clair leads an annual wilderness training program at the Gould Academy in Bethel, Maine. This is their first book.

Index

AMC Book Updates

AMC Books strives to keep our guidebooks as up-to-date as possible to help you plan safe and enjoyable adventures. If after publishing a book we learn that trails are relocated or route or contact information has changed, we will post the updated information online. Before you hit the trail, check for updates at www.outdoors.org/publications/books/updates.

While hiking or paddling, if you notice discrepancies with the trail description or map, or if you find any other errors in the book, please let us know by submitting them to amcbookupdates@outdoors.org or in writing to Books Editor, c/o AMC, 5 Joy Street, Boston, MA 02108. We will verify all submissions and post key updates each month.

AMC Books is dedicated to being a recognized leader in outdoor publishing. Thank you for your participation.

AMC BOOKS & MAPS

EXPLORE THE POSSIBILITIES

The Appalachian Mountain Club

Founded in 1876, the AMC is the nation's oldest outdoor recreation and conservation organization. The AMC promotes the protection, enjoyment, and wise use of the mountains, rivers, and trails of the Northeast outdoors.

People

We are nearly 90,000 members in 12 chapters, 20,000 volunteers, and over 450 full time and seasonal staff. Our chapters reach from Maine to Washington, D.C.

Outdoor Adventure and Fun

We offer more than 8,000 trips each year, from local chapter activities to major excursions worldwide, for every ability level and outdoor interest—from hiking and climbing to paddling, snowshoeing, and skiing.

Great Places to Stay

We host more than 135,000 guest nights each year at our AMC Lodges, Huts, Camps, Shelters, and Camp-grounds. Each AMC Destination is a model for environmental education and stewardship.

Opportunities for Learning

We teach people the skills to be safe outdoors and to care for the natural world around us through programs for children, teens, and adults, as well as outdoor leadership training.

Caring for Trails

We maintain more than 1,400 miles of trails throughout the Northeast, including nearly 350 miles of the Appalachian Trail in five states.

Protecting Wild Places

We advocate for land and riverway conservation, monitor air quality, and work to protect alpine and forest ecosystems throughout the Northern Forest and Highlands regions.

Engaging the Public

We seek to educate and inform our own members and an additional 1.5 million people annually through AMC Books, our website, our White Mountain visitor centers, and AMC Destinations.

Join Us!

Members support our mission while enjoying great AMC programs, our award-winning *AMC Outdoors* magazine, and special discounts. Visit www. outdoors.org or call 617-523-0636 for more information.

THE APPALACHIAN MOUNTAIN CLUB
Recreation • Education • Conservation
www.outdoors.org

More Books from the AMC Experts

Backcountry Skiing Adventures:
Classic Ski and Snowboard Tours in Vermont and New York

BY DAVID GOODMAN

This guide features two dozen classic ski and snowboard tours, including the highest peaks in Vermont and New York, plus the best snowboard routes, equipment, and backcountry riding tips, topographical maps for each tour, and more.

ISBN: 978-1-878239-70-9
$14.95

Backcountry Skiing Adventures:
Classic Ski and Snowboard Tours in Maine and New Hampshire

BY DAVID GOODMAN

From Mount Washington to Katahdin, discover the world beyond long lift lines. This essential guide includes tour descriptions; length, elevation, difficulty, history, and geography; topographical maps; and more.

ISBN: 978-1-878239-64-8
$14.95

AMC Guide to Outdoor Leadership
BY ALEX KOSSEFF

Fusing his own extensive leadership experience with that of acclaimed experts, Kosseff explores critical topics such as effective decision making, group dynamics, risk management, awareness and attitude, and environmental impact.

ISBN: 978-1-929173-21-1
$15.95

AMC's Complete Guide to Trail Building and Maintenance, Fourth Edition
BY THE STAFF OF AMC'S TRAILS DEPARTMENT

This expert manual includes everything you need to plan, design, build, and maintain trails—including recommendations for protective gear and choosing tools, strategies for working with land owners, and the latest techniques.

ISBN: 978-1-934028-16-2
$19.95